Big Dreams
From Small Spaces

52 Devotions for Young Women
Who Want to Change the World

Group
Loveland, Colorado

Group resources actually work!

This Group resource incorporates our R.E.A.L. approach to ministry. It reinforces a growing friendship with Jesus, encourages long-term learning, and results in life transformation, because it's

Relational
Learner-to-learner interaction enhances learning and builds Christian friendships.

Experiential
What learners experience through discussion and action sticks with them up to 9 times longer than what they simply hear or read.

Applicable
The aim of Christian education is to equip learners to be both hearers and doers of God's Word.

Learner-based
Learners understand and retain more when the learning process takes into consideration how they learn best.

Big Dreams From Small Spaces

52 Devotions for Young Women Who Want to Change the World

Visit our websites: **group.com** and **group.com/women**

This resource is brought to you by the wildly creative women's ministry team at Group. Choose Group resources for your women's ministry and experience the difference!

Unless otherwise indicated, all Scripture quotations are taken from the *Holy Bible*, New Living Translation, copyright © 1996, 2004. Used by permission of Tyndale House Publishers, Inc., Carol Stream, Illinois 60188. All rights reserved.

ISBN 978-0-7644-8843-6

10 9 8 7 6 5 4 3 2 1   21 20 19 18 17 16 15 14 13 12

Printed in the United States of America.

Contents ⭐

Contents cont.

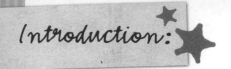

Don't Give Up On Your Dreams!

> **"Do not despise these small beginnings, for the Lord rejoices to see the work begin."**
> —Zechariah 4:10

Big dreams start small. They may start as a simple daydream, a conversation with a friend, or a note in a journal. More than an impulse, dreams have a way of drilling into our hearts, causing us to weep, talk fast(er), and obsess about how—and why—we should be chasing our dream at all costs.

You may be dreaming of finding work that matters, a relationship that lasts, or a way to serve God that will make a real difference in the world. You may even feel frustrated or impatient, ready to live your dreams but feeling limited by your circumstances. Maybe money's an issue. Or you have to finish school. Or you have young children at home. That doesn't mean your dreams are unattainable!

The stories in this book, from women *just like you*, remind us that with a little faith, a little effort, and a little help from our friends, *anything* is possible. We *can* change the world, or at least our little corner of it. We just need someone to believe in us, to encourage us, and to remind us that God is bigger than our dreams.

Included are 52 devotions, enough to last you a year if you only read one a week (but we won't discourage you from reading them more quickly)! Each includes a Bible passage and a reading, as well as a "Take a Step" idea to nudge you into action right away.

And mixed in with these devotions, you'll find "Coffee Talks" to help you talk about what you're learning. Use them when you and your friends get together for coffee (or breakfast, lunch, dinner, dessert…you get the idea!) or as a small-group study.

Throughout the book, you'll also find creative but simple ideas to help you put your personal stamp on the place you call home. These tips will help you make your space an inspired and beautiful place to live.

As you connect with God—and your girlfriends—through the pages of this book, we hope you will be inspired to dream even bigger dreams. Take a small step of faith today, and just watch what happens…

"Now all glory to God, who is able, through his mighty power at work within us, to accomplish infinitely more than we might ask or think."
—Ephesians 3:20

Big Dreams From Small Spaces

> "You have been faithful in handling this small amount, so now I will give you many more responsibilities. Let's celebrate together!"
>
> —Matthew 25:23

I remember the place well. It was just a few miles from campus. Two bedrooms, one bath, with a fenced yard. It was a castle compared to the married-housing barrack we'd been living in! It was perfect. Well, almost. A previous tenant had decided to wallpaper the one bathroom with contact paper. Orange, flowered contact paper. I knew—although we were renting—that contact paper had to go.

Shortly after we moved in, I got to work. You can imagine the labor involved in ripping that old stuff out. I used adhesive remover, my blow dryer, steam, a putty knife—anything I could think of to get that horrible stuff off of the walls of that tiny bathroom. I worked until my shoulders ached. I finished after about three days, and while they were nowhere near perfect, they were better than they were when I started. Then I got busy putting up the lovely pale blue and green striped wallpaper I had found on clearance. It was beautiful!

I felt like I had conquered the world when I was finished. I would turn on the light and just admire my work. It made me feel connected and at home, even though I was actually 600 miles from home. I learned that regardless of whether I was renting or owning, I could make my space better. I could leave it better than it was when I got there. Now that's always my goal when I move to a new place.

That's true of life, isn't it? We all want to leave the world a better place. To make it brighter or prettier; more just and good. To share God's love and grace even in small ways. Whether that means painting those bright green walls in your first apartment to make it your own, reaching out to your neighbors, or finding ways to serve your community. Wherever we are, let's strive to leave things better than we found them.

| Sue Brage |

Take a Step

Pick one small change you can make in your space. Maybe you can paint a wall, add an area rug, or make some new curtains. As you work, pray about how you can leave the world a better place just by being in it.

Take Bigger Steps

> "You saw me before I was born. Every day of my life was recorded in your book. Every moment was laid out before a single day had passed."
> —Psalm 139:16

My freshman year in college, I attended a leadership orientation for my scholarship group. As is typical with these types of events, we got to partake in a variety of icebreakers. One such task, though relatively simple, proved amazingly hard for me.

Picture this: you and a partner are outside. Small balls on the ground. Your partner directs you to the balls, and the object is to throw the balls to tag the other players out by listening to your partner's instructions. Oh, and did I mention you're blindfolded? Well, you are. As are the other people you are trying to tag. Since I went first, my partner actually had to lead me out of the room where we were meeting to the playing space outside.

Here's where I ran into my problem. I couldn't see. I didn't know what to expect next. Any step could be my last (not really, but just play along). The next step could plunge me into a huge, gaping abyss.

Even with my partner leading me by the elbow and reassuring me I was on solid ground, I literally could not tell my legs to take bigger steps out to the yard. I was taking little baby steps. My partner eventually dragged me the rest of the way down the path. Why would I be telling you this?

This is a message the Lord has been driving home to me through a variety of circumstances. Even if we can't see or think one moment ahead, he has already been there and back again.

I was slightly appalled at how even though someone was telling me, "Hey, it's okay, take bigger steps," I absolutely refused to take bigger steps for fear of plummeting to the ground and making a fool of myself. This seemingly inconsequential scene has stuck with me and provided an encouraging picture that no matter what dreams or plans are before me, God is worthy of our trust.

God has beautiful, fulfilling plans for you. It's OK if they are just beyond your grasp or above your comprehension…they're supposed to be! Isaiah 55:8-9 says: " 'My thoughts are nothing like your thoughts,' says the Lord. 'And my ways are far beyond anything you could imagine. For just as the heavens are higher than the earth, so my ways are higher than your ways and my thoughts higher than your thoughts.' "

Can't you just hear the Lord saying, "Hey, it's okay. I am right here. Take bigger steps"?

| Samantha Maloy |

Take a Step*

Tape a 6-inch ruler to a regular 12-inch ruler, and place it on your desk or nightstand to remind you that God always takes bigger steps than you do, and that is the reason you can trust him.

When Life Gives You Lemons— or Coworkers Cause You Chaos

> "Don't sin by letting anger control you. Think about it overnight and remain silent."
>
> —Psalm 4:4

It had already been a long week at work, leading up to a big event taking place that weekend. I spent countless hours preparing all of the details to make sure everything was perfect and ready to go. Two hours before things were to get underway, I walked into one of the rooms and found everything in disarray. Someone had moved all of the tables. The materials were scattered on the floor. The presentation materials were all mixed up. The chairs were completely missing from the room. I was so furious, I wanted to cry. I worked so hard, and people were on their way! My mind was consumed with questions. Who had done this? Didn't everyone know I was setting up this space?

In the limited amount of time I had until the event started, I had to make a choice. I could track down the source of my anger and frustration and make sure they knew exactly what they had done. Or I could use what little time I had to prepare the room again. I chose a third option. Since there were no chairs, I sat down on the floor and cried. Then I took a deep breath, got up, and put things back together. By the time people arrived, while things were not perfect, the event went smoothly.

Anger is an emotion that plays itself out in each person's life differently. Some of us have tempers that flare easily. Some of us rarely get angry. But we all have triggers that send us into a state where we do things we will regret only minutes later. Had I sought out the source of my frustration that day, I would have yelled and said things I could never have taken back. By the time I saw the rest of my coworkers the next day, I was no longer angry. I was just grateful that the event had gone well.

Finding a way to manage my anger and frustration that day changed how the rest of my day went. More importantly, it made a difference in how I treated the people around me. We do not look much like Christ followers when we are red-faced and yelling about chairs and papers being out of place. However, when we treat others with the grace God treats us with, his mark on our lives is unmistakable.

| Tricia Hamilton |

Take a Step

Be ready for the next time anger overtakes you. Take a small piece of paper, and write a prayer that you can say: "God, I am angry. Please help me not to sin in this anger." Put the paper in your wallet, and when you feel like exploding, pull it out and ask God to help you through that moment.

> **"Then God looked over all he had made, and he saw that it was very good!"**
>
> —Genesis 1:31

Moving away from home for the first time was exciting, scary, and sometimes overwhelming. For once, no one was telling me what to do or when to do it. The freedom screamed for big dreams and grand schemes to celebrate its existence. The entire world beckoned, and my journey into it began with my first-ever plane travel from Arkansas to Germany. No point in starting with a small hop to another state—I flew from the nest into another country.

Germany awaited, with a new language and customs. I dove into each with optimism and youthful energy. I'd never lived anywhere as small as my basement apartment. Sure, I'd shared a bedroom with my sister, but that room was within an entire house. Here, one room served as living room, dining room, and bedroom. The kitchen was so miniscule that when opened, the tiny European refrigerator door grazed the cabinet beneath the sink. A narrow bathroom completed the ensemble. Quickly the space closed in on me and threatened to squash my dreams before their roots were established.

In response to my need for room and to keep my dreams alive, I soon developed the habit of grabbing my camera and taking off on foot to explore the town and countryside. My introduction to Germany began with face-to-face encounters with half-timbered houses ("fachwerkhausen"), a trotting horse, and grape vines. These daily jaunts quickly nurtured a love for the German country and its people. My spirit lifted through the exercise and close-up connection with my new town, and my dreams found space to grow.

Every new living environment offers opportunities and challenges. Small ones sometimes require finding ways to expand. Physical walls can protect us and provide a home life, but beyond those walls is where we can find ourselves. Look outside, see what awaits you, and jump into it.

| Pamela Trawick |

Take a Step*

Look around your new neighborhood, and find a way to explore it. Step through your door and stroll within your comfort zone—to the corner, around the block, or to your local park. No matter how small you think your apartment is, relief and delight are as near as your Nikes.

Get together with one, two, or even more of your girlfriends, and celebrate your friendship. Here's stuff to do together.

★ Take time to share which of the devotions you read in the past few weeks was most meaningful to you, and why. It's OK if you all are at different places in the book—just share what God is putting on your heart.

★ Share an area of your life that you need your friends to be praying for you. And listen to the needs of your friends so you can pray for them. Remember to keep these confidential. Write each person's name and one word beside it to prompt you in prayer for her this week.

_____

_____

_____

_____

★ Go for a walk. If the weather's great, go outdoors. If it's not so great, head to a mall, the gym, your church, a school, or anyplace where you can walk and talk indoors. Enjoy sharing life together.

Tourist Trappings—Next time you visit your hometown, stop at a local attraction and pick up some postcards or kitschy souvenirs. Place them around your place or on the back of the front door to remind you of home.

> **"God decided in advance to adopt us into his own family."**
>
> —Ephesians 1:5

I'll never forget how lonely I felt the first time I moved away from home. I married my high school sweetheart the summer after we completed our undergraduate degrees, but we remained in our hometown for the next two years to complete our master's degrees.

As young 23-year olds, he joined the Navy as a medical entomologist and I tagged along as a military wife and elementary school teacher, and we journeyed to our first duty station in Jacksonville, Florida, more than three hours from any other family member. The small two-bedroom duplex on base was very plain—white walls, terrazzo floors, no curtains, no blinds. We weren't allowed to paint the walls or make any changes to the home, and we couldn't afford elaborate window dressings, having just finished grad school.

My husband and I were close to both of our families, and we missed them terribly. I decided the next best thing to being with our families physically was to have constant reminders of their love and prayers for us.

I carefully spent some of my teaching money on stand-alone picture frames and photo developing, and I embellished each piece of furniture that had a flat surface with a family member's smiling face. Suddenly my stark house didn't seem as lonely, and it became our first home away from home. Those beautiful faces especially comforted me during my husband's frequent deployments.

My pictures accompanied me to new duty stations, each assignment taking us farther from our loved ones. The pictures served as reminders of the families God carefully chose for David and me and also reminded me that I would always be part of God's family.

| Julie Lavender |

Take a Step

When was the last time you actually printed out pictures? If it's been a while, scroll through your phone, Facebook, and Instagram account and select your favorite shots of family and friends. Create a collage with some pretty paper, or purchase an inexpensive frame. Put their smiling faces up so you can see them when you aren't online.

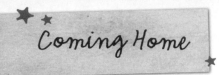

Coming Home

> **"And he will be called: Wonderful Counselor,
> Mighty God, Everlasting Father, Prince of Peace."**
> —Isaiah 9:6

What does your dream home look like? I think it's a fascinating question to ask women because we have so many different answers. Some want sleek and modern, some want a small farmhouse with acreage, some want a charming Victorian, but almost everybody has an idea of what they'd choose if money were no object. Still, although the homes we dream of may look as different as we do, the heart of what we want them to be is pretty consistent across the board—warm places where loved ones are together, laughing and happy, peaceful and secure. There's good food and good company, lots of fun and conversation. It's a beautiful picture.

The problem is that sometimes it's an image we can't seem to turn into reality. We can spend lots of money in an attempt to create those enticing scenarios, but eventually our homes seem too small or too big, too clean or too dirty, too worn or too new, and they just don't fit the image we have in our heads. Sometimes the house itself can seem perfect, but what goes on inside of it falls woefully short of the ideal; it can feel tense and cold, unfriendly and unsafe, empty and lonely. Inside a beautiful house, we can still long for peace and comfort.

I think a closer look at the Hebrew word *shalom*, however, can help us solve this discrepancy between what we long for and what we live in. The definition of *shalom* is commonly given as "peace." But I've learned it's really a multi-faceted word encompassing much more than that. It comes from a Hebrew root word that also means (among other things) "friendliness," "welcome," "safety," "security," "perfection," and "wholeness."

The idea of *shalom* has connected to it all the wonderful things that we associate with our English word "home." And what I really love is that in Isaiah 9:6, the prophesied Messiah (whom we know as Jesus) is called the Prince of Peace, or the Prince of *Shalom*. That makes him the "home" that we've all been looking for. In him we can find peace and friendliness, welcome and safety, perfection and wholeness; in him we can truly come home.

So if your home isn't all you wish it could be, or even if it is, remember that your dream home isn't in a house, it is really in Jesus; he is the only one who can fulfill everything that you long for, the one who can make your dreams come true.

| Laurie K. Schuett |

Take a Step*

From a magazine, clip a picture of a home you'd love to live in. Stick it in your Bible at Isaiah 9 to remind you of your true Dream Home.

Just Do the Next Thing

> **"We can make our plans, but the Lord determines our steps."**
>
> —Proverbs 16:9

With glossy eyes and a drowning mind, I survived my first writer's conference. My dream of writing had been planted nearly 15 years earlier and was finally taking root. As the seedling was just bursting through the soil, a deluge of rain, like a fierce spring storm, overwhelmed me.

Speaker after speaker flooded my mind with well-intentioned, expert information in the field of publishing. "Build a platform." "Show, don't tell." "Start accounts in every social media outlet; track your stats, and keep up with them." "Develop your character." "Write out your plot." "Find an agent." "Self-publish." The list went on and on, with pros and cons and conflicting advice. I had opened my mouth wide, and it was being filled to overflowing. Drowning in the information overload, I was paralyzed. I had no idea where to begin this journey.

So I did absolutely nothing! Like any seedling, a hard spring rain is good if you let it soak in. So I sat and waited and soaked and allowed all the voices to calm, the advice to get filtered in my mind, until I was quiet enough to hear God.

"Don't do it all...just do the next thing. Just do what I put in your hand to do." And I began to pray these words: *"May the favor of the Lord God rest upon us (me) and establish the work of our (my) hands for us (me)—yes, establish the work of our (my) hands"* (Psalm 90:17, NIV).

I expected my established work to be a grammar course or a writer's critique group. My next step was simple and appeared unproductive. I started simply by speaking out the dream: "I am a writer."

I thought I needed to know the exact kind of tree that was growing. I wanted to know where every branch would hang and how many seasons it would take to become this tower of strength and productivity. But what I couldn't see was the seedling developing strength, not from what was growing above the surface, but from what was growing below the surface. Soaking, waiting, listening, and doing the next small step were developing my roots. God needed me to be willing to take just one step at a time, no matter how small or insignificant it seemed.

| Cheryl Meakins |

Take a Step

Take out a piece of paper, and create a timeline of your dream. Mark and label each step you have taken. Maybe you haven't started yet—allow yourself to imagine what it will look like as you move forward. Then ask the Lord, "What is the next step or the next thing you have placed in my hand to do?"

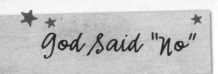
God Said "No"

"Be tenderhearted, and keep a humble attitude."
—1 Peter 3:8

Twice in the last five years, I've been pretty discouraged in my work for God. Once I started a prayer group but had to shut it down because of scheduling conflicts. More recently, I tried to start a Bible study out of my home, and despite many commitments, no one ever showed up!

It definitely makes me question my intentions. After my heart has jumped through hoops of disappointment like a trained tiger in a circus, I wonder if pursuing these dreams—that I thought were God-given—were just exercises of pride. I could chalk them up to not working out because it was wrong place, wrong time, the enemy got in the way, or I wasn't ready. But in the end, God can overcome anything, so I've had to accept he just said no.

I was raised to live my faith, to show others a different way than the way of the world, and how to deal with disappointment is part of the lesson plan. How I handle when God says "no" is part of my learning curve. When God says no, it doesn't change who he is or how much he loves me. It doesn't change God's compassion for my disappointment. It also doesn't change his greater plan for my life.

When God says no, it's because he is so good. He loves me too much to let me have lesser things—things of my own design that will not, in the end, fulfill me. God wants me to have life, abundantly, full of his grace, provision, and peace. Sometimes I need a gentle hand turning me around, making my heart tender because it's long been full of pride. Unfortunately, the only cure for pride is humbling.

I take these examples (and many others) as opportunities to mature, rather than get mired in disappointment. God isn't punishing me but is giving me another chance to experience real love. It is in the "no" that I find my "yes" to his love, no matter what. I could let the "no" stop me, or I can surrender to God's will and deal with my emotions. I might be let down, but I can be assured that he understands. In the end, when I choose to be a willing part of what he has planned, even if I have to wait, I'm making forward progress in my faith.

| Amy Vogel |

Take a Step

Look back at the times you've struggled or failed. Were any of those times an opportunity God took to say no because he had something better in the future? As you think through the past, pray that God will give you another opportunity to see him at work, giving you the best.

Coffee Talk 2

Get together with one, two, or even more of your girlfriends, and celebrate your friendship. Here's stuff to do together.

★ Take time to share which of the devotions you read in the past few weeks was most meaningful to you, and why. It's OK if you all are at different places in the book—just share what God is putting on your heart.

★ Share an area of your life that you need your friends to be praying for you. And listen to the needs of your friends so you can pray for them. Remember to keep these confidential. Write each person's name and one word beside it to prompt you in prayer for her this week.

_____

_____

_____

_____

_____

★ Have a shoe party! Invite your friends to bring a pair of canvas shoes to decorate. Supply fabric paint, brushes, and a few ideas from the Internet. Take pictures when you are done. Discuss the question: What does it mean to "walk a mile in someone else's shoes," and what can we learn from this?

Make It Yours — Monograms are a simple way to make a space feel like home. Wooden blocks or scrabble tiles are perfect. Or get an assortment of paper mache letters at the craft store, and paint them to match your décor.

Housekeeping 101

> **"Without oxen a stable stays clean, but you need a strong ox for a large harvest."**
>
> —Proverbs 14:4

Five more minutes! Five more minutes!

I scurried from room to room, making sure everything was perfect. After all, they were going to be here in *five more minutes*.

Not naturally a neat and orderly person, when company was due I always had major work to do. I would spend the day cleaning and scrubbing. I certainly wouldn't want them to think my house got messy. What would they think of me?

Then one fall, my grandparents came to visit. I intended to scrub the house from top to bottom. I even planned to organize what I affectionately call the *hall closet-of-death*. (If you go in, you might not find your way out. If you're anything like me, you know the type.) But the week got short, the days shorter. Alas, when they arrived, I hadn't even vacuumed the guest room.

"Grandpa! Grandma! I'm so glad to see you!" I welcomed them in and shut the door behind them. "I'm so sorry I didn't get a chance to clean up," I said hurriedly. "I really intended to. I planned on getting your room all set up, and I promise to get it done. How about by the time you go to bed? You see, I had such a busy week. First, I spoke at a women's Bible study, then my neighbor needed my help, then I had to…"

"Bre'anna," my grandmother calmly interrupted. "We are not here to see your house. It's a pretty house—don't get me wrong." She put both of her hands on my shoulders. "We are here to see you."

I was pleasantly surprised. I guess I had never thought of it that way. *They're here to see me. They know I'm not perfect—and that my house will get messy. What am I trying to prove anyway? That I have it all together? That I have the perfect life because my floors are mopped?*

Grandma went on, "When I was younger, I would hate it if anyone came to my door and my house wasn't in perfect order." She shook her head. "Then one day, as I ran around my house before company arrived, I thought 'Why am I doing this? My house isn't even mine. It's God's. He gave it to us to live in and use for his glory—not to burden us.'"

Proverbs 14:4 says *"Without oxen a stable stays clean, but you need a strong ox for a large harvest."* Unfortunately, I was worrying more about impressing others with my spit-shined stall than I was using it to care for and bless God's harvest—his people.

My grandma gave me life-changing wisdom that day: We are simply to use what we've been given to serve God and serve others—not to neglect it or obsess over it.

| Bre'anna Emmitt |

Take a Step

Put a sticky note on your vacuum that reads: "Use this tool to clean your floor, but serve God's people even more."

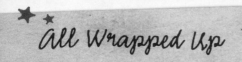

> **"This I declare about the Lord: He alone is my refuge, my place of safety; he is my God, and I trust him."**
>
> —Psalm 91:2

It should have been easy. I had a small package to mail to a friend, but I was missing the right kind of paper to wrap around my makeshift box so that it could actually survive the trip.

I hunted. I searched. I cleaned out closets. I tried cutting a brown shopping bag down to size, but it came out too small. I was getting frustrated. Such a simple thing—mailing a package. Such a frustrating roadblock—not having the proper supplies.

I remembered some hot pink wrapping paper I had stashed away. *She loves that color*, I said to myself, and got out the roll. *Wow*, I thought, *this will catch some attention in the mail room!*

The first wrap around the package looked gorgeous, but the paper was so thin I knew it wouldn't hold up. Thinking maybe a double layer would do the trick, I grabbed the edge to get a larger piece. As I unrolled it, out came the stiff center paper that was the core, the innards, the hot pink's support system.

It was sturdy. It was thick. It was brown. It was exactly what I needed.

That's the interesting part. Who knew that underneath the bright color that caught my eye was the material I was really seeking—what I'd been searching for all along. I had to get to the end to find it, but when I did, I knew it was the answer.

How often do I wrap my life in the pretty stuff, trying to hold it all together, when actually what I am depending on is too thin to adequately enable me to make my journey? If only I'd strip away all the surface material that just looks nice but actually serves no purpose, I would get to my heart, my core, the "me" God created, and realize that he was there all along and had always been supporting me. He made me, he made my dreams, and all I need to do is trust him.

And that's exactly how I want my life wrapped.

| Beth Coulton |

Take a Step

Cut a square of wrapping paper from one of your rolls. On the back write "It's what's inside that counts." Place on your fridge or bulletin board as a reminder that God loves you just the way you are, regardless of the wrapping!

Snail-Mail a Hug

> "Whatever you give is acceptable if you give
> it eagerly. And give according to what you
> have, not what you don't have."
>
> —2 Corinthians 8:12

I dreaded my sister's phone call. There had been too many doctors, too many tests, and her future now hinged on this final biopsy. For months I'd prayed for a miracle, but as the final diagnosis drew near, I felt my hope slip. Even knowing that God's way is perfect didn't deaden the heartache when I picked up the phone and heard Summer's voice.

"It's cancer," she said. "But the doctor is hopeful that surgery, chemo, and radiation will take care of it."

I was angry. Angry for Summer. Angry that her doctors had taken so long to make a diagnosis. And angry at God. But most of all, I was angry with myself. I couldn't even be there to show Summer how much I cared.

"I'm praying for you," I said, wishing I could book a seat on the next flight out of Seattle and show up at her doorstep in North Carolina with a hug, a meal, and strong hands to help her do what her own body could no longer accomplish.

By the time I was finally able to visit, Summer's beautiful hair had all fallen out. I cried when I saw her. My baby sister was weak and frail, but her strength in spirit amazed me. I hugged her, not wanting to let go.

Shortly after my return home, a figurine in a storefront window grabbed my attention. The artist's carving of two women embracing reminded me of Summer and me and how much I missed my sister. When I couldn't be there for Summer's next round of chemo, I wrapped up the statue and mailed it to her.

A few weeks later, while I was struggling through a difficult situation of my own, the doorbell rang. My mailman surprised me with a package. Inside the box lay the statue and Summer's note saying she was sending a hug back to me.

Our statue, dubbed "The Hug," accumulates frequent snail-mail miles as it travels back and forth between us. It has become our stand-in, a physical reminder of our longing to be there for one another when the realities of life prevent us from doing so in person.

I still regret the inability to be with my sister whenever I long to, but I thank God she's only a hug away.

| Dawn M. Lilly |

Take a Step

Showing you care long distance doesn't have to cost more than you can afford. If finances prevent you from sending a card, flowers, or a gift certificate for pizza delivery, print out a Scripture verse and decorate it. Let the recipient know you're praying for her. Not artsy? Find something tangible to express your feelings. Use a permanent marker to write "HUG" on a pebble and drop it in an envelope and into the mail. Your gift will say it all.

Help Me Forgive Me

> "Then he says, 'I will never again remember their sins and lawless deeds.' And when sins have been forgiven, there is no need to offer any more sacrifices."
>
> —Hebrews 10:17-18

Have you ever done something you regret? Something that hurt someone else, that got in the way of your plans, or that was just plain embarrassing? And did the memory of that one impulsive act or harsh word nag at you, always at the back of your mind, making you question all the decisions you made thereafter?

I once made the decision late at night to buy something more expensive than I could rationalize, that I knew I wouldn't need, and on a credit card I knew I shouldn't use. The morning after, despite having discussed the purchase with someone I trusted and having told myself I could learn from my mistake, I labeled myself an impulsive shopper. Going to the store for groceries or browsing an online shopping site was suddenly an evil, a temptation for an out-of-control spender. My credit card bill only reinforced the distrust I had for myself when I saw that ill-planned charge. I, who had until then managed my resources so carefully, was altered forever by this one late-night decision. Or so I thought.

It took several weeks before the uneasiness subsided and I began to separate my identity from the poor choice I had made. God showed me that I hadn't changed who I was by this one misstep. I could still be a good steward of my money. In fact, I could be even more careful, now that I knew not to make financial decisions too close to bedtime.

He also brought me comfort by reminding me that my one choice was small in comparison to my life and, even more importantly, to the vastness of his grace. The reassuring words of Christ—"I will remember their sins and lawless deeds no more"—have made self-forgiveness possible in my heart, for the big and the little mistakes, for the rest of my life.

| Elizabeth Pfotenhauer |

Take a Step⋆

Take a dry erase marker (or lipstick!) and write the words "I AM FORGIVEN" on your bathroom mirror. Every time you are tempted to beat yourself up for something you did, say them out loud and thank God for his total forgiveness and unconditional love.

Coffee Talk 3

Get together with one, two, or even more of your girlfriends, and celebrate your friendship. Here's stuff to do together.

★ Take time to share which of the devotions you read in the past few weeks was most meaningful to you, and why. It's OK if you all are at different places in the book—just share what God is putting on your heart.

★ Share an area of your life that you need your friends to be praying for you. And listen to the needs of your friends so you can pray for them. Remember to keep these confidential. Write each person's name and one word beside it to prompt you in prayer for her this week.

_____

_____

_____

_____

_____

★ Invite your friends over for a face-to-face Pinterest Party. Have everyone bring their iPads, laptops, or phones, and spend an hour on Pinterest sharing photos, ideas, and pinning each other's finds. To wrap up, ask each girl to share their favorite pin of the night and what that picture represents to her.

*DIY Art—*Purchase 12x12 scrapbook papers in colors you like. Affix to foam core or canvas and arrange on your wall as a headboard or wall arrangement.

She Delivers More Than Mail

"Work willingly at whatever you do, as though you were working for the Lord rather than for people."

—Colossians 3:23

Six times every week, I can hear the rev of the motor as the little jeep rounds the corner and heads down the country road, making its way toward my driveway.

It's the sound of our mail carrier arriving—a woman who brings so much more than just a stack of daily mail to my life. In the years that I've lived here, this woman, whose name is Kerrie, has found a special place in my heart. I pray for her, and I thank God for her.

My dog recognizes the familiar sound and runs to the road, where she is greeted by a pat on the head, a dog treat, and a flow of kind and loving words. And so I run, chasing after the dog, hoping to catch Kerrie before she leaves the mail in our box. If she sees me in time, I get a smile and my own dose of love and kindness—an always uplifting, short conversation. She takes a small piece of her day and gives it to me. I can tell she's begun spreading joy long before reaching my house; at the stop before ours, a homebound woman has received her mail, not just in the box but into her home, and oftentimes a short visit too.

I think about Kerrie and wonder what this world would be like if we all treated our daily commitments like she does. How many of us really work as though our efforts are for the Lord? Do we go the extra mile or just do enough to get by? When the Bible tells us that whatever we do, whether in word or deed, that we are to do it with thanks and in the name of Jesus, do we take those words to heart? What an impact we could have if we did. God cares not only about our daily work but also our attitude toward it because a good attitude is honoring to him.

And almost as quickly as she arrived, Kerrie takes off again, traveling on to continue her work. She is headed to deliver more mail, and more joy, to folks down the road.

| Brook Hickle |

Take a Step

Make a list of the people you come in contact with every week—at the gym, coffee shop, on the bus, in your fav take-out restaurant. You don't need to know their names! Now take the list in your hand and ask God to open doors for you to encourage them this week.

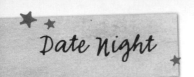
Date Night

"You have captured my heart, my treasure, my bride. You hold it hostage with one glance of your eyes."

—Song of Songs 4:9

As I write this, I'm well into my third year without a date. It's not that I'm not open to dating or that I'm too busy. There have simply been no offers. Not a confidence booster for a young woman looking forward to marriage.

On a particularly lonely Friday night, I mustered up the courage to ask God why I had been dateless so long. I expected he would tell me that he wanted me to learn patience or that the young man he had in mind simply wasn't mature enough yet—something that a little time or human effort could cure. The answer I got was very different from any guesses I made or hopes I had. God made it clear that he simply wasn't ready to share me with someone else yet.

Most people who grow up in church hear about "intimacy with God." The Bible is full of analogies that compare our relationship with God to a marriage, but we rarely get the message that God is not only able to create a deep relationship with us but he wants to interact with us on this level daily. He calls us his beloved, asks us to love him with our whole being, and offers us the ultimate sign of adoration: the giving up of his very self in order to restore our relationship with him.

Knowing that God is captivated by me and has given me this time to know him better, my time out of the dating world now has new purpose. I've started seeing someone. His name is Jesus.

| Elizabeth Pfotenhauer |

Take a Step*

This week, find a way to cultivate closeness with God. Meet him for coffee with a Bible and journal in hand. Write him a love letter, and save it to read when you feel far from him. Or ask him to take you to one of his favorite places, and wait for a word from the Holy Spirit. Anything to let him know you're interested.

Four-Legged Grace

> **"For just as the heavens are higher than the earth, so my ways are higher than your ways and my thoughts higher than your thoughts."**
> —Isaiah 55:9

Sometimes we make decisions and have no idea what we have gotten ourselves into until it's already done. That's what happened to me one cold January day at a run-down gas station.

I had just started my first real job and moved away from everyone I knew. It seemed like a great idea to have a furry companion share my new place and new life. I met a woman with two puppies at that gas station in the middle of nowhere. I was immediately smitten with both of them but knew I could only take one. The woman pointed at one and said, "This one will be happy to sleep by your feet and keep you company. The other will always keep you busy and will go with you wherever you go."

I decided on the sleep-by-your-feet dog and put her in my car. As I was about to leave, I suddenly changed my mind. I ran back to the woman and asked if I could switch puppies. She laughed and said, "Oh, you're in for it, honey!" I was thrilled with my new keep-you-busy companion and named her Grace. I had no idea how prophetic that woman's words were.

Grace filled my tiny home and new life. She was my constant companion, coming to work with me almost every day and always under my feet at home. I was sure she was the smartest and cutest Labrador ever born.

At four months old, Grace had a seizure. I had never seen anything like it and was terrified that I would lose this sweet animal God had entrusted to me—my only real confidante in my new world. I didn't lose her that day but began a long and harrowing journey of seizures, strokes, and endless medication. She turned out to be exactly what the woman at the gas station promised—a dog that would keep me busy and would go wherever I went. She is older now and still beside me all of the time. She has taught me more about unconditional love than any two-legged friend I have ever had.

That cold night at the gas station, God knew which dog I needed for the road ahead of me. Our dreams are often muted and pale when compared to the vibrancy of the plans he has for us. For me, God's plan included learning about grace and love from a keep-you-busy puppy that was not named Grace by accident.

| Tricia Hamilton |

Take a Step*

Choose your favorite worship song that focuses on God's grace. Make this your theme song this week. When you listen to it, remember that God knows what's best for you all the time!

Big Dreams From Small Spaces

A Yearly Reminder of the Bigger Picture

> **"For our present troubles are small and won't last very long. Yet they produce for us a glory that vastly outweighs them and will last forever!"**
>
> —2 Corinthians 4:17

I took a deep breath and tried to distract myself with the BMI chart on the wall of my gynecologist's office, assessing if I really fell under the "overweight" category or if I could pass as "normal." If sitting in the waiting room minutes earlier wasn't embarrassing enough, the instruction to strip everything waist down and wait for the doctor while staring at a breast examination chart almost put me over the edge. At least they gave me a paper gown to cover up with while I sat on the crunchy paper. Even at the gynecologist's office, I felt the need for modesty.

After a gentle knock at the door, the doctor entered the room and immediately detected my nervousness. Although I replayed the importance of yearly screenings and cancer prevention through my mind, all I could think about was how uncomfortable I felt and activities I would rather be doing on my sunny Tuesday afternoon.

Nothing outside of complete sedation could have made my first "woman's checkup" comfortable. While I had entertained thoughts of canceling the visit for weeks leading up to the appointment, my doctor's calm reassurance reminded me that my momentary discomfort and embarrassment would ultimately keep me healthy. That was the bigger picture.

God uses every circumstance in our lives to teach us about him, and that includes the yearly visit to the gynecologist's office. Although situations may arise that bring anxiety and fear, many times perseverance through them only increases our faith and hope in him.

| Danielle Burgess |

Take a Step

Be intentional about staying healthy by scheduling a yearly woman's checkup. As you mark your calendar with the appointment date, think of other ways God might be using your momentary discomforts to ultimately bring him glory.

Coffee Talk 4

Get together with one, two, or even more of your girlfriends, and celebrate your friendship. Here's stuff to do together.

★ Take time to share which of the devotions you read in the past few weeks was most meaningful to you, and why. It's OK if you all are at different places in the book—just share what God is putting on your heart.

★ Share an area of your life that you need your friends to be praying for you. And listen to the needs of your friends so you can pray for them. Remember to keep these confidential. Write each person's name and one word beside it to prompt you in prayer for her this week.

_____

_____

_____

_____

_____

★ Throw a tapas party! Invite your friends over to make your favorite appetizers together. Enjoy the time of fellowship and fun. Spend a few minutes at the end of the evening sharing what God is doing in your lives.

Take-Out Menu Board—Find a memo board in a fun pattern. Hang it in your kitchen or near your front door to corral your take-out menus and coupons. It's pretty...and useful!

Help! I need a new Brain!

"I love God's law with all my heart. But there is another power within me that is at war with my mind. This power makes me a slave to the sin that is still within me. Oh, what a miserable person I am! Who will free me from this life that is dominated by sin and death? Thank God! The answer is in Jesus Christ our Lord."

—Romans 7:22-24

"Help! I need a new brain!"

That seems to be the saying around here lately, coming from the innocent mouth of my 5-year-old princess. You see, even at such a young age, she's discovered that sometimes her brain/thoughts cause her to do things she doesn't want to do. I seem to have that problem too—acting impulsively, selfishly, angrily, greedily, jealously, and the list could go on and on.

That's the thing about kids. They have the ability to simplify a quite complicated problem. Here's a glimpse of the conversation I had with my daughter this week.

"It's freaking cold in here!"—Daughter

"What did you just say?"—Me (shocked)

"It's freeeeeeeaakin cold in here!"—Daughter, with a more exaggerated response

"That's a bad word. Don't say 'freaking.' Where did you learn that?"—Me

"I don't know. My brain just told me to."—Daughter

"Well, tell your brain not to say that anymore. I don't like that word."—Me

"I guess I need to just get another brain." —Daughter

I couldn't help but laugh at how simply she solved this problem. But really what got me thinking is how much as humans...we really do need a new brain. Let me explain.

In my own life I've found that my best attempts at behavior modification have miserably failed. The first two areas that readily come to mind are my desire to be more patient with my children and less easily irritated or angered. I can have others hold me accountable, try harder, and implement success techniques, but rarely am I successful when relying on human efforts alone. In fact, most of the time when my own efforts fail, I'm more frustrated than if I'd never tried because I have guilt added on to my feelings of incapability.

If you're looking for a "change factor," it can be found in Jesus alone! He is the one who enables us to change. It is my relationship with God that helps me change from my natural tendencies (impurity, selfishness, fits of rage, idolatry, just to name a few) into that which I desire to become (patient, loving, joyful, forgiving). It's a process, daily—and one which I am far from perfecting.

The truth is, I really do need a new brain! But I realize how futile my own efforts are and how closely I need to cling to Jesus to become who he's called me to be. And it took my 5-year-old to teach me that.

| Christina Stolaas |

Take a Step

Wear a hat, headband, or hair clip today to remind you of the importance of renewing your mind to God's Word. Read Philippians 4:8 if you need ideas on what to think about!

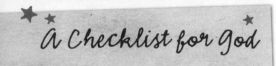
A Checklist for God

> **"The thief's purpose is to steal and kill and destroy. My purpose is to give them a rich and satisfying life."**
>
> — John 10:10

I love checklists! Anyone else? I love the thought of writing down everything in my head that needs to get done. What I love even more is the *thrill* of taking my pen and crossing off each task that I have accomplished. It makes me feel good about myself. It makes me feel like what I do matters. It makes life a little easier because I know that no matter what's going on, I can always make a checklist and accomplish something.

I wish my relationship with God could be like a checklist. He would tell me exactly how to feel, where to go, and what to do. I could write those things down, and as I did them, I could check them off. Then I would know that my relationship with him is good, that I'm doing the right things, that he loves me.

Unfortunately, when I try to make a checklist for my relationship with God, I always end up empty. I don't get the same *thrill* of checking things off of my list when it comes to my relationship with God. There's still something left to be desired; there's still something left "to do." I think that's because God doesn't want my checklist. God doesn't want me to see my relationship with him as a list of things to do. He doesn't want me to try and fit my relationship with him into my life like some chore. He wants my relationship with him to *be* life.

John 10:10 says, "The thief's purpose is to steal and kill and destroy. My purpose is to give them a rich and satisfying life." For sixteen years I've tried to make my relationship with God work using a checklist. I'm pretty sure it's robbed me of life, "a rich and satisfying life."

Today it's time for me to put down my checklist. It's time for me to stop seeing my relationship with God as something that can be "achieved" by checking things off of a list. God doesn't want my "checks"; God wants *me* so that he can give me life. So will you join me today? Put down your checklist and your pen, and tell God that you're ready to receive his promise from John 10:10. Then…let's get ready to live!

| Jenn Cross |

Take a Step

Take the next hour and forget about your to-do list for the day. Ask God to lead you in what he would have you do for the next 60 minutes without checking anything off of your list. Share your experience with a friend, and encourage her to do the same thing!

> **"I pray that from his glorious, unlimited resources he will empower you with inner strength through his Spirit...Now all glory to God, who is able, through his mighty power at work within us, to accomplish infinitely more than we might ask or think."**
>
> —Ephesians 3:16, 20

Perhaps your job is one that makes constant demands on your creative powers. Maybe in your company there is ever-present pressure to come up with something new, something fresh, and something first. Maybe it feels like eventually your source of creativity will run out.

My last semester in college, every one of my five classes focused heavily on writing, but in different ways: feature writing, blogging, literary critique, film philosophy, and mass media theory application.

I was also teaching six classes a week at my dance studio, and that meant six separate dances I needed to choreograph, all while keeping in mind the ages and skill level of my students.

There were many points in the semester that I thought I was going to run out of ideas, out of thoughts, out of words to say. And it wasn't a good feeling.

I have good news. *We* are not supposed to be the end of our source. Whether it is creativity or peace or wisdom or whatever, as Christians, we have access to a well-supplied spiritual bank account, of sorts, in Jesus Christ.

God has a limitless supply of energy, creativity, inspiration, strength, discernment, patience, and whatever else we may find ourselves needing throughout the day, and he invites us to draw from his supply as often as we need.

The more that is asked of you, the more you must ask of God. When demands are being made on you, withdraw from your spiritual bank account. You can depend on there always being funds. I can attest that God did, in fact, provide just the thought or idea I needed at every point along the semester!

| Samantha Maloy |

Take a Step*

Find a jar or bottle you can fill with sand, bath beads, or jelly beans! Fill it up to the top. Pray and thank God that he is more than able to fill you with everything you need when you need it.

Know When to Say "No"

> **"Before daybreak the next morning, Jesus got up and went out to an isolated place to pray."**
> —Mark 1:35

I remember distinctly the year that I learned to say "no." It was the year that I'd gone back to college to earn my teaching credential in music. I'd been a good student twenty years earlier when I earned my bachelor's and master's degrees in music.

But now I was a busy wife and mother of three elementary-age children. Piled on top of the normal busyness of being a mother were the added responsibilities of running my own private music studio, singing in the worship ministries at church, directing the children's music theater program, partnering with my husband to shepherd the young-married flock, practicing my own music for performance, and maintaining an active social life.

My day began at 5 a.m. and did not stop until I dropped, exhausted, into bed at 10 p.m. Everything that had to be done got done. I even spent quality time with the children. But you've probably guessed that with this kind of hectic schedule, something has to give.

And you'd be right. I was too busy to pray. Oh, I prayed on the run. But there was little time to sit, reflect on Scripture, and spend quality time with my Heavenly Father in prayer. The very thing that I needed most—*and that God desired most from me*—became the last thing on my daily agenda.

Needless to say, I grew crabby and impatient. My blood pressure went up, and my patience went down. By mid-term of my first semester at the university, I knew what I had to do. I had to say "no" to lots of good things so I had time for the most important Person.

So I taped a piece of paper next to the telephone. On it, in large red letters, it read "No!" In smaller letters underneath, I'd written "Pray first."

That big red-lettered "No!" next to the phone helped me remember to always put God first. He needs to be my number one priority. When he's not, everyone and everything else seems to get jumbled up and confused.

I've never forgotten those hectic and unpleasant first few weeks back at school. It remains a powerful lesson to not let activities—even good activities—get ahead of my relationship with God.

| Dena Netherton |

Take a Step

Make your own list of priorities, and place them on your refrigerator. Read your list each day, preferably out loud! Maybe you need to make a "NO" note to put near your phone or computer to remind you to live according to your priorities.

Coffee Talk 5

Get together with one, two, or even more of your girlfriends, and celebrate your friendship. Here's stuff to do together.

★ Take time to share which of the devotions you read in the past few weeks was most meaningful to you, and why. It's OK if you all are at different places in the book—just share what God is putting on your heart.

★ Share an area of your life that you need your friends to be praying for you. And listen to the needs of your friends so you can pray for them. Remember to keep these confidential. Write each person's name and one word beside it to prompt you in prayer for her this week.

_____

_____

_____

_____

_____

★ Schedule a movie night! Choose something in theaters you've been wanting to see...or stream something at home. Make it uplifting and funny. Afterwards, share why laughter and friendship is important in your life and what it teaches you about God.

Photo Spot— Cover an inexpensive bulletin board (check thrift stores) with burlap. Use black push pins to hang recent photos of you and your girlfriends.

Three Ice Cubes

> **"Think of ways to encourage one another to outbursts of love and good deeds."**
>
> —Hebrews 10:24

*S*adly, I tossed it in the trash. The tag said my gorgeous orchid plant required just three ice cubes a week…seemed simple enough. I'm a bit embarrassed to say that the last petal of the gorgeous, amethyst-colored flower dried up and fell off. Busyness kept my mind away from this simple, three-ice-cube task.

No big deal, right? I still subconsciously must have recognized this dead plant as failure, for the thought crept into my mind, "I am no good at this!" I snickered to myself—*it is just a plant*. Yet these three ice cubes seemed to raise up three words inside my head. And with these three words came feelings that echoed inside me as I dropped the dead plant in the garbage…*inadequate, incapable, and incompetent.* As I threw the plant away, I realized I had also thrown away my confidence.

Do you ever feel "No good at this"?

A sweet, encouraging girlfriend gave me the orchid plant; but as I threw it away, I ironically thought of the people in my life that criticized more than encouraged.

God intends for us to live with confidence and encourage one another. I know this and felt that the Lord was bringing me back to the three words that echoed in my head: *inadequate, incapable, incompetent.* Then I remembered times when God nudged me to jump *in*, speak *in*, or step *in* and help another. I'm about as good at this as I am at watering my plants sometimes.

We can lovingly step *in* and help another by simple words of encouragement; words that change *in*adequate to *adequate*; *in*capable to *capable*; and *in*competent to *competent*.

As I came in from throwing away the orchid plant, I passed by my flower garden outside, which just happens to need more than three ice cubes a week; thankfully, it's on its own watering system. Like you and me and our circle of girlfriends, there were some thriving flowers and some wilting flowers. Like the flowers, some of us are flourishing and thriving—maybe someone remembered their three ice cubes…ha-ha!

Like flowers, we grow with helpful soil, and we help one another "outburst" from the soil by watering with our words of encouragement. You never know when your words will come to mind to help and keep them from throwing away their confidence. They may just need three ice cubes a week.

| Julie Lane |

Take a Step

Is there someone in your life that appears to be wilting from lack of encouragement? Take the time to write them a note with three things you appreciate about them as a way of watering their soul.

Dream Big, and Cast Away Fear!

> **"For God has not given us a spirit of fear and timidity, but of power, love, and self-discipline."**
> —2 Timothy 1:7

As a young college student, I took a preaching class to overcome my fear of public speaking. Although I have always loved people, I have struggled with this fear all of my life. I took this preaching class because I wanted to learn to preach and I wanted to use my teaching gift more effectively. We were assigned three different Scriptures for three sermons that semester. My first two sermons were okay, but being the perfectionist I am, I felt like I'd done horribly. I remember crying after my first sermon, thinking I had failed.

I set up a meeting with my professor and shared my frustration with him. His response to me was, "Lynda, you are a natural-born speaker. People want to listen to you." No one had ever said that to me before. Was I truly gifted? Perhaps there was truth to this. He was, after all, a pastor. If he saw potential in me, perhaps I really was good.

After hearing my professor's words, I decided to make my final sermon my best! I truly wanted it to be less about my own insecurities and more about God. I called my final sermon "Dream Big, and Believe That God Is Faithful." After preparing and praying for an entire week, I preached the sermon to my class with a passion and fervor I had never seen before.

I was elated when my classmates said it was the best sermon that had been preached in our class all semester.

My professor commended me for smiling during my preaching and made me an example to the entire class. I couldn't believe what I was hearing. Did the girl with the fear of speaking in front of big crowds really preach to a class of twenty-plus students? Were they truly moved by my words?

How many times do we underestimate ourselves and allow fear to hold us back? Often the way we view ourselves is not accurate with the truth of God's Word, but merely a collection of false belief systems we've acquired through life. All of us are guilty of believing negative things about ourselves and even doubting God when he calls us. God knew what he was doing when he called you and me. Trust him to lead you to the right places.

| Lynda Hanna |

Take a Step*

Create a new Pinterest board entitled "No Fear." Add pins of things you would like to try but have been afraid to in the past. Ask God for courage and opportunity to try some of them!

61

Mud Comes Before a Fall

> **"Pride goes before destruction, and haughtiness before a fall."**
>
> —Proverbs 16:18

As the rain poured and mud splashed the sides of the radio station's white van, our promotions team shivered under soaked sweatshirts and umbrellas meant for listener giveaways. Even the screen-printed tent with the station's call numbers and tagline wasn't holding back the rain very well. Visions of water bursting through the seams in a very coach-drenched-by-athletes moment played through my mind. The only place I wanted to be was home.

The forecast hadn't cooperated with our team's plans of promoting the soft rock station at the county fair that day, but advertising contracts forced us to stay in the muddy mess for the full two hours. As I brushed wet strands of hair out of my eyes, I struggled with the reality that my glorious, albeit unpaid, internship with one of the city's top radio stations was falling very short of my high expectations.

The allure of backstage passes to free concerts and festivals all summer long had been enough to make me quickly apply and take the position. My ego swelled as I shopped for famous recording artists coming into town and formed relationships with disc jockeys known throughout the city. Dreams of working in a high-profile career shadowed the pride building in my heart. But as the rain poured and the mud splashed, I didn't only realize how prideful I'd become; I realized that my idolized career in radio was not the plan God desired for me. I was back to the drawing board.

Sometimes we can be so tempted by what the world offers through power and position, we lose sight of God's plan for us. We start down paths that we create and find ourselves at a loss when expectations aren't met and fallout occurs. We must make sure that our dreams are God's dreams and that pride doesn't build up in our hearts as we strive to make our mark on the world.

| Danielle Burgess |

Take a Step

Do you have a pride problem? Here's a quick check: review your latest Facebook and Twitter posts. Are they self-centered and boastful? Or can they be used to minister and help others? Determine that for the next seven days you will post only what encourages and lifts others up…not yourself.

Grateful for Losing It All

> "And we know that God causes everything to work together for the good of those who love God and are called according to his purpose for them."
>
> —Romans 8:28

I had big dreams. I thought a college degree would make me important and fulfilled. But 10 different jobs in 12 years, each related to the other but not quite "it," was leveling the "big dream" hopes I used to have. I felt lost and frustrated. I was going nowhere in life. Until the season that God allowed a Job-like experience to happen to me. I lost my job, my condo, had to move back home to each of my parents' homes (they are divorced), and had to file for bankruptcy. I was devastated and embarrassed. I had to start all over!

My turning point arrived when a good friend asked me to do some public relations for him. I had no education or background in publicity or marketing. But what I did possess was the desire to learn and to try something new. I agreed, and after a short time, landed him an interview and placement in a local publication. This was a light bulb turned on in my "lost" world. Turns out I had a knack for publicity!

Today, I am building my PR company. I'm not huge (yet), and I have a lot to learn. I don't drive a fancy car or own a home, and I don't shop at high-end luxury stores. But I am doing something I love, and I am using (and discovering) the gifts God has given me.

God allowed me to lose so much in order to gain him and his perspective. Though it was not fun to be unemployed and not be able to pay rent, God made me depend on him alone. Today, my "lost-ness" is a testimony to encourage, motivate, and demonstrate to other women and entrepreneurs God's faithfulness, compassion, and power. Like Joseph (in Genesis), what seemed like evil against me, God turned around for my good.

Maybe you feel totally lost or on the verge of giving up. Do you know that those heart's desires may have been planted by God himself? Sometimes he uses discomfort to spur you on to use the gifts he has given you. Step out of the boat and into the water with Jesus. He's got you.

| Donina Ifurung |

Take a Step*

Write down your big dreams and aspirations, seal them in an envelope, and place them in a drawer. Tell God that you are trusting him with every hope and dream you have and placing your future in his hands!

Coffee Talk 6

Get together with one, two, or even more of your girlfriends, and celebrate your friendship. Here's stuff to do together.

★ Take time to share which of the devotions you read in the past few weeks was most meaningful to you, and why. It's OK if you all are at different places in the book—just share what God is putting on your heart.

★ Share an area of your life that you need your friends to be praying for you. And listen to the needs of your friends so you can pray for them. Remember to keep these confidential. Write each person's name and one word beside it to prompt you in prayer for her this week.

_____

_____

_____

_____

_____

★ Head out for coffee! Whether it's a latte or a cappuccino or you opt for a cup of tea, take time to savor the flavors of your warm drink as you savor time with your girlfriends. (And think about inviting someone new to come along! It's a nonthreatening way to get acquainted.)

Picture Your Dreams—Grab some old magazines, and select photos that represent the dreams you want to pursue. Mount them on coordinated cardstock to place on the front of your fridge. Add some fun magnets, and you have a personal and inspiring display every time you open the fridge!

Keep Your View Clear

> **"Commit your actions to the Lord, and your plans will succeed."**
>
> —Proverbs 16:3

I live in a condo. It's about 1100 square feet. It's not a tiny space, but it's certainly not large! I've learned that especially in small living spaces, it's important to be creative and keep the rooms feeling open and uncluttered.

I read in a magazine once that it's particularly important to keep your view clear in a small room. You want to remove limits visually—to make the space seem larger than it really is. Any number of creative elements can help accomplish this. Things like glass tables can open up a room and make borders vanish, or using a single color on the walls will unify a space. These optical illusions create the feeling of limitlessness in a small space.

This really resonated with me. I started looking at my space to see if I had anything that was making it feel smaller, anything that was cluttering up my view. As it turned out, a few small changes made a big difference!

As I reflected on this, I realized this principle is true in my relationship with Jesus, too. When I let things clutter my view of him, my "space" and life seem so much smaller than they really are. I feel closed in and pressured. As a result, I feel much less contented and peaceful in my heart.

The beautiful thing is, just like in my condo, when I do clear my vision and lose the boundaries, my mind and heart start to relax. My relationship with Jesus becomes the focus, and the stress and other things lose their hold on me.

I need to be reminded to clear my view to let his light in. I need to realize that my space—no matter how big or small—is exactly where God wants me to be. Jeremiah 29:11 says: "'For I know the plans I have for you,' says the Lord. 'They are plans for good and not for disaster, to give you a future and a hope.'"

What an encouraging word! He knows the plans, and he knows where I'm going, each and every step of the way. When I remove the barriers, I can see him more clearly, and my relationship with him grows brighter.

| Emily Thompson |

Take a Step

Look around your space today. Maybe you are in a small condo, a dorm room, even an office cubicle. Would you say your space feels clean and clear...or cluttered and confined? Choose one action you can do today to clear your view. Maybe you can sort a pile, get rid of something, rearrange the furniture, or open (or remove) the blinds. As you work on your project, ask God to help you see him more clearly, too.

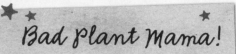
Bad Plant Mama!

"For he satisfies the thirsty and fills the hungry with good things."

—Psalm 107:9

I have this plant.

I can't remember the name of it, but it was gorgeous when I got it. I nurtured and cared for it, watered it, gave it food and light. Then one day, it started to look saggy. It must need more water, I thought. So I watered it, and it looked worse.

It must need transplanting, I thought. So I went to the store and got an adorable planter. I put my plant into it, watered, and waited. No luck. It still didn't look good. And I was at the end of my green-thumb ideas.

Quite by accident, I forgot all about the poor plant. Life got busy. By the time I remembered that it might need some water, the plant's soil was rock hard, but...the whole plant looked better. Perkier. That would be crazy backwards, I thought. Dry plants don't grow.

So I watered it some more. And you can guess what happened.! A few days later, it looked like the sun had beaten the life out it. Finally, I got it! Over the next few weeks, I resisted the temptation to douse it from the watering can as I watered my other plants around it. It broke my heart to ignore it, but I forced myself to walk away without so much as a drop. I couldn't even cast a glance its way; I felt like a bad plant mama.

When I could stand it no longer, I got in close to inspect how my experiment was going. I took a long, hard look at my poor potted child, and what I saw in the crumbling, caked soil was large shoots of new growth, fresh leaves, and newly formed buds ready to bloom. The existing foliage was looking greener than ever, and instead of draping lazily over the edge of the planter waiting for certain death, the flowers from before were starting to spring to life and heading towards the sky again.

Leaving it alone turned out to be the best thing I could have done for the plant. The parched soil was enabling life and growth to thrive.

How often we are there. Life can be dry sometimes—a lot of the time. We think we are spinning our wheels, just waiting to be watered again. But, oh my, what's happening in us and in our hearts during the desert spells is something only the divine Gardener can do. That's when we learn the most and the best about God and how awesome he is.

We cry out for rain, but growth can happen in the hard rocky soil of our lives and our days. And amazingly, we flourish.

| Beth Coulton |

Take a Step*

Buy a small cactus plant for your living space. Use it to remind yourself that faith can grow even in the driest desert times of our lives.

—1 Peter 2:18

*S*tarting in my new job as an outside sales rep was daunting. I was a top performer in the inside group, but to suddenly be selling "in person" was not only a big leap for my career, it was a big leap for my emotional maturity. It got more harrowing when I realized the man just promoted to be my boss didn't like me or my sales style. I was far from his top pick for this position, and for months, it felt as if he was doing everything he could to help me fail.

At the same time, I had just started back in my relationship with the Lord. One day, during a venting session, a dear friend revealed to me what was really going on under the surface of my work situation. It was a test. Not the kind of test you get graded on, but certainly one I would pass or fail. It wasn't whether I would meet the goals I was hired to achieve, but rather, a test of my faith—if I would obey God. In treating this man with humbleness and respect, I would win him over God's way. If I continued to bristle at his authority, I would not succeed spiritually or professionally. It was my first real, tough choice as an adult Christian.

My friend suggested I pray for my boss. Initially I was more than hesitant. But it ended up making all the difference. Without (daily) lifting him up, I would not have been able to make it through the eight months in his employ. I wasn't a doormat, but I was respectful and tried to lean into his knowledge. My prayers were often simple, such as "Lord, bless him today," or they were for me, "Lord, if I have to talk, help me to be nice."

It was a complicated time, but eventually, the heat was off. While we never became friends, my boss and I learned to work together well. Now that I have moved on, the lesson God taught me—to follow him through respecting those above me—makes it possible for me to have an authentic faith in the workplace, as a wife, in a Bible study, or in the PTO. The lessons we learn through testing often have the biggest impact.

| Amy Vogel |

Take a Step

Write down the names of three people in authority over you. Pray for them this week...and see what happens.

Wide-Mouthed Women

> "For it was I, the Lord your God, who rescued you from the land of Egypt. Open your mouth wide, and I will fill it with good things."
>
> —Psalm 81:10

Are you waiting for something but not receiving it? Do you know that you're meant for something more, but nothing's happening?

I recently came across a verse that, when I read it, the words jumped off the page, clicking into my mind and filling another gap in the big picture of who our God is and how he works. My perspective of God's generosity was shaken up. It was Psalm 81:10: "For it was I, the Lord your God, who rescued you from the land of Egypt. Open your mouth wide, and I will fill it with good things."

According to this verse, my part was simple! Open my mouth. God's part? Filling it. When we do our part, God will do his. Obedience is what's needed. God is saying, "I have already done such good things for you. Open up and let me do more!" Is your life open wide to him…or are you holding your plan in your hands, expecting him to come in and work within it? He wants us to come to him open and empty.

This is what I call being a "wide-mouthed" woman! What does it mean? Be surrendered, holding out your arms to him. Don't hold back. Don't sell yourself short and miss out because you're not opening up wide enough to him. Be receiving. Be ready. Be open.

Surrender is the key. Give your dreams to him, and he will come in and work. When we are open to him, he can fill you with good things. It's going to take work, but remember that he *asks* us to open our mouths, our hearts, our lives to him. When we do, he promises to give us his life—life that is satisfying, savory, nourishing, and filling.

| Chesli Hutson |

Take a Step*

Choose a wide-mouthed jar or vase, and fill it with flowers. If you don't have access to fresh flowers, gather some twigs or branches and make a centerpiece for your table. As you enjoy your creation, let it remind you that God wants to fill you with his life.

Coffee Talk 7

Get together with one, two, or even more of your girlfriends, and celebrate your friendship. Here's stuff to do together.

★ Take time to share which of the devotions you read in the past few weeks was most meaningful to you, and why. It's OK if you all are at different places in the book—just share what God is putting on your heart.

★ Share an area of your life that you need your friends to be praying for you. And listen to the needs of your friends so you can pray for them. Remember to keep these confidential. Write each person's name and one word beside it to prompt you in prayer for her this week.

_____

_____

_____

_____

_____

★ Go on a bike ride with your friends. Get back to nature with a trail ride, or head downtown on your bikes for a day of window shopping and chatting. Grab smoothies while you share one dream you want to accomplish in the next 12 months.

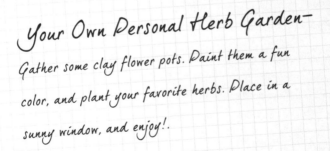

Your Own Personal Herb Garden—

Gather some clay flower pots. Paint them a fun
color, and plant your favorite herbs. Place in a
sunny window, and enjoy!.

> "Keep putting into practice all you learned
> and received from me—everything you heard
> from me and saw me doing. Then the God of
> peace will be with you."
>
> —Philippians 4:9

My checking account dwindled. Due to poor planning, I had less than a hundred dollars to last me until the end of my first semester of college. Christmas was coming, and there were still presents to buy plus the usual living expenses. How could I be excited about the "most wonderful time of the year" when my car tank sat on empty?

Alone and depressed, I strung lights on my dollar-store tree. As my fingers worked through a tangled strand, an image came to mind. It was of the cross. I remembered how growing up, Christmases past had been a lot leaner. As a child, my parents still made the holiday meaningful by reminding me of the true meaning of Christmas.

I let go of the lights and paced my room, searching for a sheet of paper. A leftover neon pink poster board sat on my desk. I grabbed a pen and began sketching a cross. The shape became as wide and tall as the poster before I cut it out.

Pushing the tree away from my window, I raised the blinds. The cross fit perfectly in my oversized window. A few pieces of tape held it in place.

As I resumed decorating for Christmas, the image in neon pink hung for all the campus to see. It was a bold witness. My simple holiday cross brought renewed hope in me, as I thought: What else could I do to bring a visual reminder of Christ for those around me to see?

| Shanna Groves |

Take a Step

Find the spot in your room you are most likely to see when you wake each morning. Whether it is hanging a cross or creating a small bouquet of pink flowers, add something to that spot that will inspire your faith, as well as those who visit you.

Tornados and Entertaining Angels

> **"Keep on loving each other as brothers and sisters. Don't forget to show hospitality to strangers, for some who have done this have entertained angels without realizing it!"**
> —Hebrews 13:1-2

It started out as a normal workday for me. I had opened up the small thrift store that I manage and was getting ready for customers. Despite the appearance of a normal day, I soon realized it wasn't going to be just another day. The sky outside grew darker by the moment, and soon the radio began blaring severe weather warnings. As the hail began to come down outside, I quickly evacuated the small storefront and made a dash for our small town's welcome center—the safest haven in a tornado.

As the tornados passed over (we lost count at three!), the welcome center collected a variety of guests and travelers from our nearby scenic byway. Two of those refugees were 20-something girls. I introduced myself and one of my co-laborers in ministry and began answering their questions about our small town, which is home to the boarding school that I work for. We quickly learned that these two young ladies, Sarah and Kaitlyn, were sisters from a neighboring state who were enjoying a camping trip before the hail and tornados waylaid them.

Outside, the storm began to lift as our foursome chatted about our town, its history, and our roles in its unique ministry. Out of nowhere, Sarah looked at me and said, "I'm just going to go out on a limb here and assume that you girls love Jesus a whole lot."

The rest of the day was a blur as these young ladies stayed to volunteer their services, toured our campus, and became a part of our lives. As we sat back to enjoy dinner together, Sarah and Kaitlyn told us that before they set out on this trip, they had been praying for some encouragement in their Christian walk. They knew just a handful of young believers and even fewer who were passionate about serving Christ in a radical way.

As we showed them to their accommodations for the evening (we couldn't have our new friends sleeping in a tent!), we marveled at what had happened that day. Out of the dozens of people taking shelter, I introduced myself to those two. Sarah asked about our faith. We offered a meal. They offered their time.

It's been over a year since that day, and Sarah and Kaitlyn still come to visit now and then. Their friendship is a constant reminder that God works in mysterious ways.

| Tekoa Miller |

Take a Step*

Take a few moments to pray that you don't miss any God-opportunities that may cross your path today.

Control Freak

**"So don't worry about tomorrow, for tomorrow
will bring its own worries. Today's trouble is
enough for today."**

—Matthew 6:34

As we welcomed them in, the house was filling with smoke. Only moments earlier I had learned that when things bubble over in a gas-powered oven, it starts a fire. Thankfully, turning the oven off solved the problem. No casserole, though, for the company.

Sarcastically I thought, "Good thing this was the first time we were having this family over. I mean, why wouldn't this be the night we blow something up?"

Later that evening we discovered one of our plates is not microwaveable. There was another near explosion and fire. Two glass bowls came tumbling from the cupboard and shattered all over the whole kitchen. Add to that the crumbling plaster on my ceiling and the fact that our pre-lit Christmas tree overheated, putting out half the lights (which happened randomly throughout the evening), and now you get the whole picture.

First impressions that we had our act together dissipated quickly as thick smoke filled the hall. Somehow, we still managed to have a good time, and the peppermint cake was actually delicious!

This is one of those times I feel God laughing at me—well, not at me…but with me. Not in a nasty, sarcastic sort of way. More in a "Stop trying so hard, this isn't the stuff that matters" sort of way.

I confess, I am a recovering Control Addict. I like to keep order with those things that I think I can. I hate chaos. Too much noise overwhelms me. I like the house clean when people come to visit. I like it when things turn out the way I want them to.

Too often I want control because I hate the feeling of falling. I want to grab hold of life and keep it close where it all will make sense. Yet, when that is the case, I will miss out. No human controlled the day that Christ came to earth, the way he lived and died and conquered death. I want relief from momentary troubles; he longs to bring eternal transformation.

God just keeps proving that I can't impress. I am not in control. I learned a long time ago that I don't want to be. Really! In the midst of our crazy evening, I learned to take myself less seriously. I laughed until my sides hurt at how ridiculous things were. I also got to explain to our new friends why our family is called to be missionaries to the inner city. When we love Christ, we give up our false sense of control...and learn to laugh in spite of it.

| Leneita Fix |

Take a Step★

Take time to watch the sunset tonight, or get up and watch the sunrise tomorrow. Reflect on the fact that God is ultimately in control of everything, and practice resting in that fact.

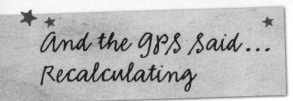

> **"We can make our plans, but the Lord determines our steps."**
>
> —Proverbs 16:9

I absolutely love the invention of the GPS. I honestly cannot even begin to imagine what my driving experience would be like in my professional and personal world without it. I suppose I'd actually have to learn to effectively read a map, plan ahead, and waste tons of gas in the process.

When I drive, I often turn my GPS on even though I am fairly certain I know where I'm going. When the GPS is on, I can spend my efforts focusing on the physical road, the other dangerous drivers out there, and the scenery. With step-by-step commands to follow, I find I can drive much more relaxed.

Sometimes, though, I purposely ignore and disobey the directions. It's usually because I'm convinced that the particular route it wants me to go isn't necessarily the most effective or desirable. If you use your GPS in familiar areas, I'm sure you're guilty of the same thing. After all, since I'm physically here in this city, I do know certain shortcuts that the GPS doesn't quite understand. What happens when I choose a different route? Thankfully, the GPS doesn't shout when correcting me. There's no demeaning voice saying "Turn around, idiot!" Nope. The authoritative and calm voice simply says "Recalculating."

Today as I was driving, I realized that God's direction for my life works in a similar way to the GPS. God desires that I focus on the driving and stay on the road instead of being consumed—or distracted—by each turn in the road or wondering what comes next.

My main job is to listen to the turn-by-turn directions from God and to trust the route. At times, the "turn left in .5 miles" doesn't make much sense. It may inconvenience me, be uncomfortable, or simply not be the driving route I envisioned to get me to the destination. However, since God is the author of my final destination, I'd say he has the knowledge to dictate the best route.

One of the things I love most about God is that when I do find myself on a detour, his faithful and steady voice simply says "Recalculating." He doesn't give up on me! He doesn't get frustrated with the fact that I made a wrong turn (again!) He simply recalculates the route from exactly where I am and desires from here forward that I will follow his directions.

Often the detour means it will take longer for me to get to my destination. I may miss out on some roadside blessings or end up driving in undesirable conditions. Regardless, God simply recalculates my life. My Faithful Father has promised he knows where he wants me to go, knows the best way to get me there; and if I simply trust him, it's going to be an incredible ride!

| Christina Stolaas |

Take a Step

Find an old map (or find one online you can print out). Cut out a piece of the map, and attach it to a 3x5 card. Draw an imaginary route on your mini map, and then stick it on the fridge as a reminder to follow God's directions for your life.

Coffee Talk 8

Get together with one, two, or even more of your girlfriends, and celebrate your friendship. Here's stuff to do together.

★ Take time to share which of the devotions you read in the past few weeks was most meaningful to you, and why. It's OK if you all are at different places in the book—just share what God is putting on your heart.

★ Share an area of your life that you need your friends to be praying for you. And listen to the needs of your friends so you can pray for them. Remember to keep these confidential. Write each person's name and one word beside it to prompt you in prayer for her this week.

_____

_____

_____

_____

_____

_____

★ Take a walk down memory lane. Pull out your photo albums, and share them with your girlfriends. Or bring your yearbooks and be ready to laugh. Talk about your best memories and also what you are looking forward to in the years to come.

Welcome Home— If at all possible, hang a wreath on your front door or put out a welcome mat to welcome you when you come home.

Beyond My Wildest Dreams

> " 'What do you mean, 'If I can?' Jesus asked. 'Anything is possible if a person believes.' The father instantly cried out, 'I do believe, but help me overcome my unbelief!' "
>
> —Mark 9:23-24

In my soul, I knew there could be no way my American-cultured comforts would say yes to a mission trip to a Third World country for ten days. My mind agreed with the reality check that we did not have $5,000 in our bank account. No passports—and I hate shots!

No matter how hard I tried to distract the pastor to a different topic, he continually brought us back. I finally looked at him and committed to praying about it and told him we would get back with him. It worked. He put away the pictures of the hungry children, and we discussed more immediate matters that needed to be dealt with.

As my husband and I drove home, I shared the reality of what I was thinking. He sat and listened. Conviction pierced my heart. "I told him we'd pray about it. Probably should, eh?"

I spent the next seven days giving God all the reasons I was not qualified to go help the hungry children or minister to pastors and their families. Then I waited for a thundering message to come give me a "yes" or "no." Only silence and peace came.

I sat my husband down one evening. "That mission trip? I think, maybe, we're to go."

"Where will we get that kind of money in such a short time?"

"I have no idea, but if we are to go, God knows the plans he has for us, and he knows how to provide for those plans. Let's send out letters to our friends and family, pray over them, and trust God with the rest."

We were in agreement. I sat down at the computer and prayed before I typed the letter. I hit "Print" and grabbed the address book. The next day we stood together. My husband prayed over the envelopes, and I took them to the post office. The waiting game began.

The next morning, before the letters could have even arrived at their destination, we received a phone call from a family member. He notified us of an inheritance coming our way. It was in the amount of $5,000 dollars. I was speechless—humbled—overjoyed. I realized that even my comfortable cultured reality cannot stand in the way of God's plans for our lives. I surrendered to his will.

I repented for my selfish pride and began rejoicing at God's plans for our future! Now it was time to reach out to others beyond the comfortable setting of our own culture.

Including God in the decision-making process helped me see beyond my comforts and the reality of my financial situation. He took me to a deeper faith and trust in him than I had ever experienced before. Every fear of the journey that rose up was replaced with a faith that with God all things are possible.

| Deborah J. Watson |

Take a Step

What is that one possibility that seems impossible you have tucked away in the back of your heart? Write it down on a small sheet of paper, and tuck it into your Bible at Mark 9. Spend the next seven days reading this chapter. Pray about your impossibility, and trust God with the answer he gives you as well as the timeline that he gives it to you.

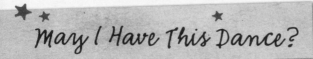

May I Have This Dance?

> "Lead me by your truth and teach me, for you are the God who saves me. All day long I put my hope in you."
>
> —Psalm 25:5

The music was soft and beautifully orchestrated. It reminded me of a lovely ballroom dance. I closed my eyes and pictured myself dancing with Jesus, gracefully gliding across the floor. We danced my favorite—the waltz!

My thoughts drifted back to the time I had taken ballroom dance lessons. How comfortable and exciting it had been to dance with the instructor. He knew what he was doing and where he was taking me! Even if I didn't know the dance, it was easy to follow his lead because of his instruction. He'd taught me to press into his left hand with my right and to press the small of my back into his other hand. By doing this, I could immediately sense his leading; with even the slightest movement of his hands, he could steer me in whatever direction he wanted me to go.

Then the revelation came: this is how the Lord desires to direct me! I am always to be facing him; his hand is in the small of my back, and as I press into him, I'll sense his leading. In pressing in to know him, my sensitivity to his Spirit's gentle nudging will increase. Then as I respond in obedience to his leading, he can steer me in the direction he desires me to go. There is a trust factor involved because I can't always see where he is taking me, but he promises to keep me from stumbling. When I am in the posture of facing him, in intimate contact, he can whisper in my ear, gentle correction or loving affirmation. *Jesus, may I have this dance?*

| RoseAnne Sather |

Put on some beautiful music…and dance with Jesus!

Perfection Not Required

"And whatever you do or say, do it as a representative of the Lord Jesus, giving thanks through him to God the Father."

—Colossians 3:17

My husband and I had only been married for about six months. We were both in college and had no money to buy Christmas presents. We decided that instead of buying gifts for our family members, we would make them cookies.

The plan was great, in theory. What I failed to do, though, was buy extra ingredients just in case a batch or two didn't turn out exactly as I hoped.

Late on Christmas Eve, I started baking. The first batch turned out great—melt-in-your-mouth goodness. But then we got to batches two and three. I don't know if it was our old oven or my lack of experience, but somehow both batches burned. And of course, it was Christmas Eve. Midnight. None of our local stores were open to buy more ingredients.

As I pulled the final cookie sheet out of the oven and saw my tar-colored cookies, I lost it. I scraped one of the cookies off of the pan and kicked it across the room in tears. My perfect plan was ruined. Christmas was ruined. Or at least that's what I thought at the time.

What I failed to realize was that perfection wasn't necessary. My family wouldn't have cared if the cookies tasted as bad as they looked. In fact, they wouldn't have even cared if we didn't bring them a present at all. I aimed for perfection when all that was really required was love.

Have you ever done something similar? We convince ourselves that our service has to be perfect. That we can't have someone over for dinner if we're not an impressive cook. That we can't sing in the worship band unless our voices are flawless. That we can't write a devotional because we might spell a word wrong. If we can't be perfect, we'd rather not even try.

How much better to do what you can with what you have...and trust the results to God. God never asked us to wait until we were perfect to serve. He simply asked us to serve and leave the perfecting to him.

| Lindsey Bell |

Take a Step

On a small piece of paper, write one way you have always wanted to serve, something you've hesitated to do out of fear of failure. On the back of this paper, write Colossians 3:17, and place it on your bathroom mirror as a reminder of today's devotion.

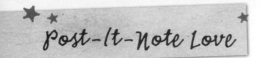

Post-It-Note Love

> "Don't use foul or abusive language. Let everything you say be good and helpful, so that your words will be an encouragement to those who hear them."
>
> —Ephesians 4:29

It was my junior year of high school, and I had just finished the last class of the day. Ready to head home, I hurriedly walked outside to the parking lot and started weaving my way through the madness of students.

As I approached the back of my little black car, I started to notice that something strange was on my windshield. Having parked in a space that I was not supposed to be parking in (and yes, I was, according to the school, illegally parked), I was sure I had received a ticket from the school and would be paying some outrageous fine or scheduling a date with the principal. It was a pleasant surprise when I made it to the front of my car to find the entire windshield covered in Post-It notes and a single rose under one of the wipers.

My boyfriend, who is now my husband, had driven from his school over a half an hour away to place a Post-It note on my windshield for every month we had been together, along with notes which described his favorite memories from our time together. To this day I still have every single one of those Post-It notes, and I keep them stored away in my memory box.

As women of God, we're lavished *daily* with love notes from our Savior. In fact, if the skies could act as our windshield, it could never be enough to hold the expanse of notes that God has written and will write for us. God just loves loving us. But how do we respond to that love? Paul urges us in Ephesians 4:29 to let everything we say be good and helpful so that our "words will be an encouragement." We need to understand and truly grasp the *power* our words have in building up and encouraging someone or tearing them down and discouraging them.

As women who are loved so greatly, how could we ever speak anything other than that which builds another up? But the truth is, so often we do. The good news is that you have a choice. From this very moment on, you can choose to speak words of love, words that encourage and build up and reflect a loving Savior. Choose love.

| Kelly Scott |

Take a Step

Take a moment to grab a Post-It note and write a genuinely encouraging note to surprise someone with today. You can choose to sign it or remain anonymous. Either way, it will be very meaningful to the person who receives it, possibly something they cherish for years and keep in their memory box. As you are writing your note, praise God for his many notes of love.

Coffee Talk 9

Get together with one, two, or even more of your girlfriends, and celebrate your friendship. Here's stuff to do together.

★ Take time to share which of the devotions you read in the past few weeks was most meaningful to you, and why. It's OK if you all are at different places in the book—just share what God is putting on your heart.

★ Share an area of your life that you need your friends to be praying for you. And listen to the needs of your friends so you can pray for them. Remember to keep these confidential. Write each person's name and one word beside it to prompt you in prayer for her this week.

_____

_____

_____

_____

_____

★ When was the last time you played miniature golf? Hit the local mini-golf course, and have a great time laughing as you play. Make up funny ways to hit the ball (with your left hand if you're right-handed, with your head hanging upside-down... you get the idea)! You don't even have to keep score. Just have fun together.

A Quiet Moment—Fill a crate, basket, or pretty box with your Bible, journal, reading material (like this book!), a pen, and some Kleenex. Set it near your favorite chair, and you'll be ready anytime you want to sit down for a quiet moment with God.

Where Did My Strength Go?

> **"Don't be dejected and sad, for the joy of the Lord is your strength!"**
>
> —Nehemiah 8:10

There it was in my hand—my 30th job rejection letter. All I could think of at that time was, why me? What is wrong with me that I got rejected? Again?

This job was perfect for me; it was an actual church job! I wanted to be in the mission field full time again. Yet at this moment I was rejected. In my tears, I was crying out to God. Yes, I even said angry words to him. I felt like I couldn't do anything. I was in utter despair.

A small voice whispered to me, *The joy of the Lord is your strength.*

What did that mean, the joy of the Lord is my strength? Are you kidding me? I had no more strength—I wanted to give up. The small voice whispered again, *The joy of the Lord is your strength.* For the next few minutes, I heard the same line over and over…*The joy of the Lord is your strength. The joy of the Lord is your strength. The joy of the Lord is your strength…*

I was trying to understand. I was feeling the furthest thing from joy right now! How could I find joy in the Lord when at that moment there was no joy to be found?

I knew I had heard of the line before and went onto one of my favorite search engines and typed in "the joy of the Lord." It was in Nehemiah. I started to remember what the Israelites went through when they found the long-forgotten Book of the Law. Here they were, crying because Ezra the priest had found the book and was reading from it. They wept as they realized how far they had fallen from God and still he never abandoned them. Nehemiah told them to stop grieving and rejoice in the Lord...for he was their strength.

That is what I needed to do! I needed to stop grieving and focus on God because he is my strength. To help my mind focus on God, I got out my journal and started writing what I liked most about God...and what was good about serving him.

The first thing I wrote was *faithful*. I love that God is faithful. Then I found a Scripture to go with the word *faithful*. As I kept writing out things I loved about God, I realized that I was finding joy in God! As I was finding joy in him, I started to get my strength back. For the next thirty days, I took time whenever I could and wrote something about God. My strength was returning because I was finding my joy in him.

| Crystal Nicole Livingston |

Take a Step

What do you like about God? Write it on a piece of paper or in your journal. Find a Scripture that goes with it, and write that down, too. Keep it for the days when you feel you have no strength...and need to find your joy in God!

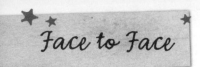
> "Inside the Tent of Meeting, the Lord would speak to Moses face to face, as one speaks to a friend."
>
> —Exodus 33:11

In the last few years, social media has become the rage. People use social media to connect to childhood friends, find college acquaintances, and meet new people. It seems the days of sitting down and having a meaningful and unrushed conversation are almost gone.

Despite the fact that people are sharing lots of information on social sites, close inspection reveals that people are really not connecting. The information shared tends to be insignificant and superficial. If we aren't cautious, this false sense of connectedness can deprive us of intimate friendships.

God designed us for relationships. In addition to our relationship with Christ, we need girlfriends who love us for who we are, give honest advice even when it is hard to hear, and hold us accountable to biblical truths, especially when we are experiencing a rough spot in the road. Relationships of this nature require connectedness that runs deeper than reading about your friend's whereabouts, retweeting the new recipe she shared, or viewing the pictures in her latest online photo album. We need to know and be known. We need to share our joys and struggles and to support each other in our faith journey.

Nothing develops friendship and connectedness more than face-to-face conversations. When you sit across the table from a friend, you have the opportunity to watch and listen. What she has to say takes on additional meaning. You see joy written on her face or read the intensity of her pain. You are intentional in asking questions and sharing words of encouragement. You offer a hug, along with wisdom. In turn, she does the same for you. Being intentional in spending face-to-face time with your friend will result in a deeper relationship.

Your relationship with God benefits in much the same way. Some days your communication with your Heavenly Father may resemble a couple of tweets. Those days are bound to happen, but God desires for you to make time to sit with him and share more than a few facts. He desires to hear what joys and struggles you are experiencing. He desires to speak words of encouragement as you travel this Kingdom road with him. He desires some time with you face to face.

| Tracie Fritcher Johnson |

Take a Step

Set the alarm on your phone to go off several times today. When it does, as soon as you are able, stop what you are doing and spend a few minutes focusing on God. Maybe you will feel led to send up praise or share a burden you've been carrying. You will find he will bless you regardless of what you bring to the table.

101

Pinterest Perfect

> **"Don't be concerned about the outward beauty of fancy hairstyles, expensive jewelry, or beautiful clothes. You should clothe yourselves instead with the beauty that comes from within, the unfading beauty of a gentle and quiet spirit, which is so precious to God."**
>
> —1 Peter 3:3-4

That appetizer is sure to be a crowd-pleaser. (Click.) Oooh! That living room is beautiful! (Click.) I would feel so pretty in that $500 dress. (Click.) If only my hair and makeup looked like this. (Click.)

These are the thoughts swirling through my mind and toying with my emotions as I scroll through photo after beautiful photo on my Pinterest account. What sounds like a harmless activity—"pinning" these photos and storing them in my electronic bulletin board of inspiration—easily turns into a heart-altering, self-bashing session. One that can cause me to lust after things I cannot afford, dream of attaining a perfection within my own home that is simply not possible, and make me feel as if I'm seriously falling short in the housewife-of-the-year department.

Don't get me wrong, I love how easy it is to jump onto the World Wide Web and quickly find a fun recipe, gather photos of decorating or party planning inspiration, and search makeup and fashion tips from professionals in the industry. But at the end of the day, my wardrobe doesn't contain cute clutches and fabulous high heels of all colors; my pantry isn't lined with neatly organized chalkboard-laden mason jars; and I don't have cute homemade banners hanging at all my parties. To put it simply, *I'm not Pinterest perfect*.

I've found that my innocent clicking and scrolling is feeding a deep (and dangerous) desire for unattainable perfection; and this lack of perfection is not only damaging to my personal life, it's intruding on my spiritual life. Maybe you've never been on Pinterest.com and you have no idea what I'm talking about. However, as a woman, I'm sure at some point you've felt less than perfect. I'm almost positive you've faced a moment where you feel you don't quite measure up to women around you or girls you see in the media.

1 Peter 3:3-4 says: "Don't be concerned about the outward beauty of fancy hairstyles, expensive jewelry, or beautiful clothes. You should clothe yourself instead with the beauty that comes from within, the unfading beauty of a gentle and quiet spirit, which is so precious to God."

Girlfriend, you are *so precious*. (I'm speaking to myself here, as well.) Let's refuse to let the magazines, TV, and what we see on the Internet (including Pinterest!) draw our hearts away from the beauty we have in Christ. Let's refocus our hearts on what truly makes us radiant. You are priceless, and nothing on this earth can make you more stunning than a gentle spirit and a heart focused on the Lord.

| Danya Collyer |

Take a Step

Grab a note card or pretty piece of paper, and write 1 Peter 3:3-4, but at the beginning, insert your own name as if it's a letter directly written to you. Place this card or paper on your laptop, near your TV, on top of your magazines, or anywhere you're tempted to worship perfection. Let this promise serve as a sweet reminder of your worth and value. You, sister, are irreplaceable and precious.

Rainbow Sightings

> "I have placed my rainbow in the clouds. It is the sign of my covenant with you and with all the earth. When I send clouds over the earth, the rainbow will appear in the clouds, and I will remember my covenant with you and with all living creatures. Never again will the floodwaters destroy all life."
>
> —Genesis 9:13-15

There are not many things more beautiful than a rainbow painted across the sky after a rain, with its kaleidoscope of colors, especially seeing its majestic arch. Even if the sky is still somewhat dark, everything appears so vivid and fresh. When I see a rainbow, it immediately reminds me of God, his promises and his provision in my life.

I love the fact that rainbows represent God's covenant with us. It's as significant today as it was for Noah and his family. God knew life would be hard and we, too, would need reminders of who he is and of his many promises. Not only does God give us his Word and his daily presence in our lives, he gives us things in this world to remind us of his eternal power and divine nature. I love knowing that God could have chosen anything, but he chose a "rainbow" to show up after a storm to give us hope and perspective.

I remember learning in school about how Isaac Newton studied and scientifically explained why rainbows exist. I understand that light is reflected and refracted and that rainbows occur when raindrops and sunshine cross paths. But when I see a rainbow, I am not concerned with the scientific explanation or even what is at either end, though I do find it interesting that God references rainbows primarily at the beginning and the end of the Bible in Genesis and Revelation. The significance of rainbows to me is that God knew we would have storms in our lives and we would need constant reminders of him; so in a unique and colorful way, he provided something in the shape of an umbrella which he called a rainbow.

Though I live in a state that does not have much rain, I see the colors of the rainbow reflected every day in various ways—when the sprinklers come on, through my glass coffee cup, in the ice in my water glass, when going through the car wash, or wherever I may be. Each time, I am reminded of God's promises, and it gives me immediate perspective. "Thank you, Lord, for your Word, your promises, and for rainbows!"

| Jennifer Sorcinelli |

Take a Step*

Take a few minutes today to look at photos of rainbows on an Internet photo site. Choose one for your computer or cell phone "wallpaper"…or make a quick slide show. Throughout the day, let these pictures remind you of the promise of God's love and forgiveness in your life.

Get together with one, two, or even more of your girlfriends, and celebrate your friendship. Here's stuff to do together.

★ Take time to share which of the devotions you read in the past few weeks was most meaningful to you, and why. It's OK if you all are at different places in the book—just share what God is putting on your heart.

★ Share an area of your life that you need your friends to be praying for you. And listen to the needs of your friends so you can pray for them. Remember to keep these confidential. Write each person's name and one word beside it to prompt you in prayer for her this week.

_____

_____

_____

_____

_____

★ Have a donation drive for your favorite charity. Find out what they most need, and invite your friends to start collecting those items. Make a plan to meet and deliver your goods together, if possible. Grab lunch, and talk about how it felt to give as a group...and brainstorm other ideas for future projects!

Special Centerpiece—Ask your mom (or aunt or grandma...) for a vase or container you can use as a centerpiece. Fill it with flowers, place it on your table or breakfast bar, and let it remind you of the special people who love you!

> **"For your royal husband delights in your beauty."**
> —Psalm 45:11

It happens around the same time every year. I get the call. I respond automatically with something like, "Oh! That sounds awesome! I can't wait!" All the while, the dread is beginning to creep in...first in my mind and then quickly making its way to the pit of my stomach. But I know what I have to do.

I begin the inevitable journey to my bedroom. Slowly, almost painfully, I slide open the dresser drawer and start pulling the source of my dread out piece by piece. It's once again time to face reality: Swimming Suit Season has arrived.

I do a miniature fashion show for myself with the three suits that I've deemed somewhat acceptable over the years. I follow the same routine every time: I stand in front of the mirror. I poke. I turn to the right. I turn to the left. I suck in. I tilt my head for a better angle. But it's useless. I always end up sprawled across my bed, cursing myself and remembering all the times I should have passed on the sweet treats and headed straight to the gym instead. All I want—my deepest desire—is to stop obsessing and feel beautiful.

Maybe it's not the swimming suit body for you...maybe it's shoes, filling your closet with different pairs in an effort to create the perfect outfit. Or maybe it's the latest makeup trends, always needing the newest shadow or looking for the perfect gloss. But no matter the way you channel your energy, isn't it true that as women, we all desire to feel beautiful? Isn't our deepest desire to know that someone sees our beauty?

If you're anything like me, often you forget there is someone who calls you beautiful. Psalm 45:11 says, "For your royal husband delights in your beauty." Let that sink in for a minute. No, really, stop and think about it. God, the creator of heaven and earth and the very source of beauty, delights in YOUR beauty. Yes, you!

The verse goes on to say: "Honor him, for he is your lord." I think God intentionally attached those two lines as a challenge to us women because he knew how our hearts would long to be called beautiful. So let's do it! Let's take the challenge and honor our amazing Lord by getting back to believing in our true beauty.

My prayer for you is that as you do this day after day, you will begin to see the light of Jesus radiating from deep inside you. I pray you begin to see and delight in your true beauty the same way your royal husband has and will for all of eternity.

| Krista Hugenberg |

Take a Step*

Go to a mirror. As you look at your face, say these words: "Jesus calls me beautiful. I am beautiful!" What was going through your mind when you did this? Write your thoughts in your journal, or share with a close friend.

Forever Hold Your Peace

> **"I am leaving you with a gift—peace of mind and heart. And the peace I give is a gift the world cannot give. So don't be troubled or afraid."**
>
> —John 14:27

My best friend recently lost her job. Overwhelmed and unsure of how to proceed, she turned to God for her comfort. Soon a divine peace overwhelmed her, and she was able to take some time for herself before starting a calm and intentional search for new employment. I listened with delight as she told me how happy she was to be free from a job that was unhealthy for her both emotionally and professionally. She could see God's hand at work in her career.

The funny thing about peace, though, is that the world does not understand it. Many of the people closest to the beautiful young woman questioned her serenity, dismissing it as disinterest or even depression. Her struggle quickly turned from a search for peace to a battle to keep it. Amid the daily barrage of questions about her situation, she prays for a good grip, a strong hold on the one thing that keeps her going: that beautiful, all-consuming peace.

In his letter to the Philippians, the Apostle Paul writes that this peace "exceeds anything we can understand" (4:7). Jesus says it's "a gift the world cannot give." Receiving this precious treasure takes a special kind of openness, but keeping it out of the hands of a cruel and ignorant world requires even more fortitude. The strength for this task comes with training and with reliance, just like my friend's, on the one who gave us our gift of peace in the first place.

If you can pinpoint a place in your heart or a part of your life that lacks the understanding-defying peace of God, take some time to lay that before him. Make it a quiet couple of minutes so you can not only present your concerns but await his promised response. Say it aloud or in your mind: "This is my gift from Christ, and you can't have it!"

| Elizabeth Pfotenhauer |

Take a Step

Find a picture that represents peace to you—maybe in a magazine, online, or one on your phone or camera. Print that out, and place it somewhere you will see it, and every time you look at it, thank Jesus for his gift of peace that goes beyond your circumstances, your thoughts, and your understanding.

> **"He heals the brokenhearted and bandages their wounds."**
>
> —Psalm 147:3

My poor golden retriever Lucy. Due to an unknown cause, she had chewed the fur off of a spot on her leg, and now her bare skin was exposed. I sensed there were going to be physical consequences if left unattended, so I took her to our vet, who gave me an alcohol spray to spritz on the area twice daily. That sounded simple enough, but this would be no small task to perform on 75 pounds of man's best friend.

The first night, I sat on the floor and called her over, spray in hand. When she sat beside me, I aimed the medicine at the bare spot and squeezed the trigger. As it hit her skin, she jumped and pulled in closer to me due to the sting of the alcohol. I knew it hurt, but I also knew I hadn't gotten enough on. I sprayed it again, and this time her pain was so great that when she reacted, she threw herself into my side so hard she knocked me off balance.

And if *she* hadn't knocked me off balance, the sheer irony of the situation would have. You see, I was the one currently responsible for her pain. But because of our relationship, she knew she could trust me and sought to find comfort in my presence. Instead of running *from* me, she sought my protection. Instead of *lashing out*, she drew closer. Instead of *blaming me*, she wanted my love.

In that moment, I thought about what I do when I sense that God is allowing some pain to pass through his hands and into my life, thus resulting in life not going exactly as I had hoped. I realized that my reaction is to run the other way; to let him know that this is not part of my plan. In times like that, I usually don't find myself cozying up to him, because I now feel life is unfair; after all, I didn't get my way. I don't usually body slam into him for comfort, love, and protection.

But according to my dog, that's exactly what I'm supposed to do.

Once I'm there close to his side (and I'm always the one who needs to move, not him), God will do for me exactly what I did for Lucy that night—put his arms around me, tell me he's so sorry but this present pain is indeed necessary, and stick right beside me until the sting goes away and I'm back on my feet again. He's always faithful to show me that a healed wound is better than an open one.

| Beth Coulton |

Take a Step

Share this story with a friend who is hurting right now. Talk with her about a time God helped you through a painful situation. Pray for her to press into God during this time.

Roller Coaster Day

> "So be strong and courageous! Do not be afraid
> and do not panic before them. For the Lord
> your God will personally go ahead of you. He
> will neither fail you nor abandon you."
>
> —Deuteronomy 31:6

A few Saturdays ago I snuck away for a "mommy" day. I spent the whole day alone at Busch Gardens Europe in Williamsburg. You'd be surprised how much mental peace you experience walking through faux Europe when no one needs *you* to do things for them. You actually complete a thought more than once during the day...who knew? A lot of soul searching and mental gymnastics gets done while riding roller coasters five times in a row. There's something about loops and drops that clears out mental cobwebs.

While I was at the "old country," I received a wonderful phone call from my son letting me know he'd been accepted into the Appomattox Regional Governor's School for vocal performance. It is quite the honor to be selected, and we had been waiting to hear for quite some time, so needless to say, I was ecstatic for him. There I was...a free day, time alone, *and* good news!

Little did I know that just hours later, my day, that previously only contained the ups and downs of roller coasters, would soon contain some other serious downs, too. I received another phone call not as full of joy as the one I answered earlier during the day. This call left me hanging like the Griffon's scary face-nearly-perpendicular-to-the-ground drop, and it produced the same heart-coming-out-of-the-chest, stomach-in-the-throat feeling. This call revealed that my dad had been admitted to the hospital and needed surgery to remove blood clots in his legs. All the unknowns, concerns, and lack of answers threw me for more loops than the Alpengeist coaster's speedy, feet-dangling twists and turns; only now I wasn't laughing, and the adrenaline rush wasn't eagerly anticipated.

Life is one wild ride, with good news and bad, ups and downs twisting hand in hand. On the coaster, you cannot have that crazy drop without the relaxing, reclining, slow but steep climb into the sun. Receiving a good phone call with great news about my son and a devastating call about my dad is typical of life's roller coaster days.

I'm glad that God wants to ride with us through it all. His Word says he will never leave us or forsake us and reminds us not to be afraid, because he is with us whether we are screaming in excitement or screaming in anguish. God's Word tells us again and again he won't leave us or forsake us. God knew that for every twist and turn our life took on this wild ride, we would need to hear it again.

Thankfully, we can continue the wild ride with confidence that we are not alone—even when things are scary. Big dreams and big goals in life often have many ups and downs. God uses the ups to encourage us and the downs to equip us and teach us to cling to him. We need both. Knowing that, we can be willing to stay on the ride and embrace both the ups and the downs.

| Stacy Decker Poole |

Take a step ★

Take a second and have a roller coaster prayer moment. Thank God for one UP in your week, and then think about one of your DOWNS and ask him for wisdom and courage to trust him with the situation, remembering that whether up or down, he loves you and will *never* leave you.

Coffee Talk 11

Get together with one, two, or even more of your girlfriends, and celebrate your friendship. Here's stuff to do together.

★ Take time to share which of the devotions you read in the past few weeks was most meaningful to you, and why. It's OK if you all are at different places in the book—just share what God is putting on your heart.

★ Share an area of your life that you need your friends to be praying for you. And listen to the needs of your friends so you can pray for them. Remember to keep these confidential. Write each person's name and one word beside it to prompt you in prayer for her this week.

_____

_____

_____

_____

_____

★ Grab a group of friends, and head to the local amusement or water park. Ride the roller coasters or surf pool. At the end of the day, talk about how your life resembles an amusement park right now and what you are learning through the ups and downs.

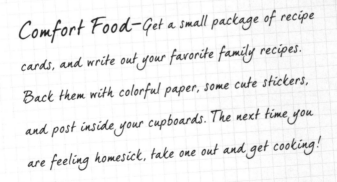

Comfort Food—Get a small package of recipe cards, and write out your favorite family recipes. Back them with colorful paper, some cute stickers, and post inside your cupboards. The next time you are feeling homesick, take one out and get cooking!

The Lesson of the Library Book

> **"The master said, 'Well done, my good and faithful servant. You have been faithful in handling this small amount...Let's celebrate together!'"**
>
> —Matthew 25:23

I tossed the mail on the table as I rushed through the door. An oversize letter caught my eye. I was surprised to find it was from the library. I mean, the book was only a month overdue, and they were threatening to file charges and report it to the credit bureau. Wow, I guess they don't mess around with delinquents like me.

I thought about the book stuffed in the back of the car, where it had been for the past three weeks while I ignored the urge to return it every time I went out. I was always too busy to stop...or it was out of the way...or I just didn't want to. The more time went by, the harder it became to do the right thing. Well, judgment day was here. I had to return the book and make this right.

Now, you may be thinking, such drama over a simple library book. Yet, there was a deeper message for me. God was nudging my heart to become faithful in the small things. You may not think returning a library book on time has spiritual implications, but for me it did. I could regale you with tales of notoriously late library books. From the time I was young, I struggled with this same scenario. I had quite a reputation at my local library, and not in a good way!

This episode was telling me something. Being faithful in something as minor as returning a library book on time mattered to God, and it needed to matter to me. The truth was, it didn't matter, and that, was the problem. I thought of the often-quoted Scripture from Matthew: "Well done, my good and faithful servant. You have been faithful in handling this small amount, so now I will give you many more responsibilities. Let's celebrate together!"

It's as if I thought this only applied to "spiritual" things like reading my Bible or praying. But in reality, those things aren't little at all. Little things are those we rationalize or excuse away. The dessert we eat when we're trying to be healthy. The extra cup of coffee when we need to cut out caffeine. The paperwork that needs to be filed or bill that needs to be paid.

I've always claimed I'm just not a detail person. However, God has called me to be faithful in small things. You know what details are? Small things.

God wasn't mad about the library book. I don't have to be perfect for him to love me. He was simply using the overdue letter to remind me that as I am faithful in the small things, he will bless the big things.

| Sue Brage |

Take a Step

Is there something you've been putting off doing? If at all possible, do it today as an offering to God, showing him you want to be found faithful... even in the small things.

Big Dreams From Small Spaces

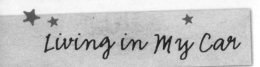
Living in My Car

> "But when Jesus heard about it he said, 'Lazarus's sickness will not end in death. No, it happened for the glory of God so that the Son of God will receive glory from this.'"
>
> —John 11:4

I live in my car. Well, not really, but it feels like a reality most days. I live in one town and commute to another town 30 miles away for school, work, and even shopping. It's been a dream to sell my house and move closer to my life. This dream has been confirmed by God on numerous occasions…yet I haven't sold my house and haven't moved.

There was a time when I became overly focused on moving, looking at houses, dreaming of furniture placement, driving through neighborhoods. It consumed my thoughts and my actions. I was out of balance. It's now been seven years in limbo, and I don't do limbo well.

I've heard the story of Lazarus in countless sermons and thought I knew it frontwards and backwards. But one detail had escaped me all these years…the timeline.

Jesus is great friends with Mary, Martha, and Lazarus.

Jesus was away and received word Lazarus was sick. Jesus said, "Lazarus's sickness will not end in death."

[What happens here??]

Lazarus dies.

Jesus takes his time getting to Lazarus. He finds out Lazarus had died and brings him back to life.

It made sense to me in the past that Jesus would say, "Lazarus's sickness will not end in death" *after* Lazarus died. But that's not what happened. Jesus said this *before* Lazarus died. My amazement lies in the [What happens here??] part of the timeline—especially from the perspective of Mary and Martha. Jesus said it would not end in death…*then* Lazarus dies. How could that be? How could Jesus lie? Death is an end; and Lazarus is dead. But of course we now know Jesus didn't lie, and he knew all along an amazing miracle was about to take place.

What do I do when my circumstances don't match what God has said? Do I panic? Do I call God a liar? Do I doubt? Do I lose all patience and try to fix it on my own? (Honestly, at one time or another I've said yes to each of those!) Instead, I need to choose to see things through God's eyes and believe what he says. Even when my circumstances directly contradict what God has said or promised, I need to hold fast to him and believe.

Can you believe I'm still saving moving boxes after all these years? It's my way of holding fast to God's promises and watching for my miracle.

| Janna Firestone |

Take a Step

Is there a situation in your life right now where you're waiting for God's words to become a tangible reality? Choose something that represents that miracle, and place it where you can see it and thank God for his promises…and his timing!

Diaper Changes Can Be Meaningful

"Whatever you do, do well."—Ecclesiastes 9:10

"Live in the moment." How often have we heard that? It's supposed to be a stress buster and good for our health. But what does it really mean? We text at meals, converse on phones while shopping, and some people game during sermons! It seems we're so busy with our daily lives, one moment blurs into the next.

Thinking about this, I came to the conclusion that the word *live* is the clue. *Live* in this sense does not simply mean breathe the air, keep the body in full faculty, and sustain your being. It's far more expansive. In my way of thinking, it means to take the present and celebrate it, eat it up, let it flow in you like a rhythmic dance, a lovely scent to breathe in.

"Fine," you say, "that's very nice, but at this moment I'm changing the baby's diapers. Hardly a celebration, and I'm desperately trying *not* to breathe in."

I know. I've been there. But nonetheless, it is a moment of life.

Often we're so busy thinking about what we need to get done this evening or what awkward situation happened at work yesterday that we fail to grasp what is happening now. Now is what we have, and not by accident. People, events, even tasks enter our daily lives, and repeatedly we give them very little heed, when indeed they are a respected part of God's design for us. He, by his gracious Spirit, is present with his children. Therefore, nothing is insignificant. Whether in the midst of a mundane situation or a life-changing event, it is ours and belongs to no one else. Embrace it.

Whatever place you are in—preparing for the Boston Marathon or sidelined by illness, raising a family or on your own, washing dishes or signing a multi-million dollar contract, and yes, even changing your baby's diapers—this is your moment. See Jesus in it, and live fully.

| Marilyn Leach |

Take a Step

What is the most "insignificant" thing you do each day? Ask God to show you how to make that meaningful…and to appreciate that task in a new way!

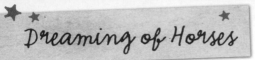
Dreaming of Horses

> "Take delight in the Lord, and he will give you
> your heart's desires."
>
> —Psalm 37:4

I had plans to graduate college and go on to a career training horses, so when I found myself living, not in a quaint log home, but in a crowded neighborhood in Southern California, I thought maybe God had forgotten me. I felt lost without my horses and the woods I'd grown up in. It was obvious we were going to be here for a few years as my husband pursued his career dreams. And even though I was lonely, I didn't pursue friendships because I was determined not to get attached.

I kept myself busy working and tried to learn how to manage my home; all the while, I was dreaming of long horseback rides and mountain air. If God really does give us the desires of our heart, why wasn't he listening?

One day a teacher I worked with learned of my love for horses. After school she introduced me to her grown daughter, Joy, another horse lover. By that weekend, Joy and I were riding in a nearby state park. I didn't know people in the city could own horses.

Despite my fears, we purchased a house close to my husband's new job, where we lived less than a mile from a dairy. I loved walking to see the cows. Not long after, my husband came home from work with good news. "My coworker knows of a place to board your horse." I marveled at the way God worked. I thanked him for remembering me even when I complained instead of trusted.

That summer I moved my horse to his new home! I continued to ride with my friend Joy in the mountains of San Bernardino County. God had bigger plans than I could imagine. He knew I needed friends more than I realized. He gave me the desire of my heart, but he also changed my heart. I learned that friends bring more than just fun into our lives; they can open doors for God to give us the true desires of our hearts. I've learned to pursue people, whether I think the friendship could only last an hour or a lifetime. Go out of your way to make a friend today even if you have other plans. Amazing things can happen.

| Jessie Gunderson |

Take a Step*

Think of a friend who has a dream she is not able to live at this time in her life. Send her a small gift representing that dream, with a note reminding her that God has not forgotten her.

Coffee Talk 12

Get together with one, two, or even more of your girlfriends, and celebrate your friendship. Here's stuff to do together.

★ Take time to share which of the devotions you read in the past few weeks was most meaningful to you, and why. It's OK if you all are at different places in the book—just share what God is putting on your heart.

★ Share an area of your life that you need your friends to be praying for you. And listen to the needs of your friends so you can pray for them. Remember to keep these confidential. Write each person's name and one word beside it to prompt you in prayer for her this week.

_____

_____

_____

_____

_____

★ Host a make-your-own-sushi night! Find some recipes (and how-tos) on the internet. Purchase (or borrow) supplies, and divvy up the ingredient list. Enjoy each other's company as you learn something new. (Have a box of frozen egg rolls on hand…just in case!)

You're a Winner—Display a piece of sports memorabilia in your space. Your old softball glove, basketball, or trophy will brighten up the place and inspire you as you remember past victories.

Nothing Ventured, Nothing Gained

"For God has not given us a spirit of fear and timidity, but of power, love, and self-discipline"
—2 Timothy 1:7

For some reason, going to get a haircut is an event full of anxiety for me. For most, getting a haircut is routine, normal, and nothing extravagant. But for me, the options and decisions of a haircut are plaguing. Days before I know that I am going, I constantly think about my haircut. How much am I going to cut off? Do I want to change the style? Should I keep my bangs or let them grow out?

As I wait for my stylist to call my name, I continue to make little tweaks to the image I have in my head, prepare what I am going to say to her, and psych myself up for this great new look that I will walk out with. When my name is called, I sit in her chair, take a deep breath—and chicken out! Instead of telling my stylist my great new look, I spit out my usual style: two inches off the bottom, and keep the side bangs. When it came down to the first snip of her scissors, I couldn't bring myself to take the plunge and change up my look.

Finally, for my latest haircut, as usual I thought and thought about what I wanted to do for days prior to the appointment. But when the fateful day came, as I waited for my name to be called, instead of thinking about my haircut, I was thinking about something that my professor had said in class earlier in the week when he was telling us what his mantra is: "Nothing ventured, nothing gained." This mantra had been in my thoughts since that class period and what it meant to me and my life. I had decided after class to adopt that mantra as something that I will live by, to take a leap of faith and trust in God in order to accomplish things I never thought I could do.

When my name was called and I sat in my stylist's chair, I took a deep breath and told her to do something completely different from my usual. I closed my eyes as she started to cut, and I repeated that mantra until the cut was over. At the end, I looked in the mirror—and I loved my new look!

Even though it was something as simple as a haircut, my new mantra helped me step out of my comfort zone and take a risk to change something in my life. This small step helped me to look for even bigger differences that I can make in the future when I trust in God.

| Sabrina Hakim |

Take a Step*

Come up with a mantra that you can apply to your life. Make it something that really hits home, like a Bible verse or quote that struck you as important. Find (or make) a piece of art you can use in your home to encourage you to live by your new mantra!

Rest Is Not a Four-Letter Word

"Be still, and know that I am God!"

— Psalm 46:10

Has God ever used someone in your life to help you learn something? My enlightened moment came while leading a mission trip for older elementary students. As the girls prepared for bed, I sat in the room pounding away on my laptop, updating parents using social media.

Allison, a fourth grader on her first trip, piped up, "Ms. Kaylea, you need to turn your computer off and go to sleep!" As I groaned, thinking of all of the things left undone, she added, "and stay off your phone!"

Rest, needless to say, is not something I do easily. Yet this is the lesson God is teaching me in a variety of ways. I've started thinking about rest as more than one word. Instead, it seems to be an acrostic for renewal, endurance, strength and time.

Renewal: Just as fuel fills up a car, rest helps me recharge for the next task.

Endurance: Rest gives me the ability to face both daily tasks and unexpected tasks.

Strength: Rest gives me stamina for the tough times. Without rest, even easy tasks seem to take additional effort.

Time: Pure and simple. In order to rest, I need to give myself a chance to unwind and relax.

Rest doesn't come easy. I have to stop and disconnect from the world. It's only when I intentionally build breathing space into my life that I am able to recharge my mental, physical, and spiritual batteries.

So much to her delight, I listened to Allison and turned my phone and laptop off and went to sleep. Maybe next time I'll remember to be still without needing a fourth grader to remind me.

| Kaylea Hutson |

Take a Step*

Right now (or OK, maybe on your lunch break) take a couple of minutes to stop, close your eyes, unplug from the world, and give yourself the gift of a few minutes of silence. Have extra time? Why not eat your lunch at the park today and enjoy?

Small-Town Girl, Big-City World

> "Remain in me, and I will remain in you. For a branch cannot produce fruit if it is severed from the vine, and you cannot be fruitful unless you remain in me. Yes, I am the vine; you are the branches. Those who remain in me, and I in them, will produce much fruit. For apart from me you can do nothing."
>
> —John 15:4-5

Standing in the corridor, having pushed the "Down" button, I heard the whir of busy elevators going up, then down again, paying no mind to my simple request. Suddenly I was overwhelmed with the isolated feeling of being a small-town girl in a BIG city. The lights outside the window stretched for miles, emphasizing my feeling of insignificance. I wanted to retreat to my hotel room, to hide in the confines that felt safe and comfortable…and known.

My new employer had sent me to LA for a conference. I was feeling a bit inept in my new job, wondering if I was really up to the challenge. My confidence was taking a beating. Now here I was in a big city, surrounded by confident, experienced professionals. The environment emphasized my feelings of insecurity; but at the same time, it forced me to my knees, seeking assurance from the only one in whom my true security lies.

My prayer that night was one I would pray often as I started my career. It focused my desire to make my life—and my job!—count for God's glory. To make a difference in the world, whether I was in a small town or a big city.

"Jesus, thank you that within your created world, I have a purpose; I'm not a faceless nonentity. You have plans for me personally. I am not insignificant. I want to make a difference in my circle of touch; to carry hope as in a water can to sprinkle a dry world; to plant a seed of joy in the window box of a sorrowful heart; to paint a fresh coat of peace over a graffiti-stained wall of unrest; to kiss a few frogs; to bring healing to a lame soul. I recognize that I'm helpless without you, Jesus. Without you, I *am* that small-town girl in a BIG-city world. You alone are my significance—only you give me value. But with you, this little girl *can* make a difference, maybe even one of eternal significance."

| RoseAnne Sather |

Take a Step

On a piece of paper or in your journal, write out your own prayer asking God to help you see your greater purpose and place in his great big world.

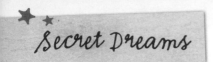

Secret Dreams

> "For the Lord your God is living among you. He is a mighty savior. He will take delight in you with gladness. With his love, he will calm all your fears. He will rejoice over you with joyful songs."
>
> —Zephaniah 3:17

As the women slipped the ball gown over my head, fitting it to my waist and making the last adjustments, silent tears gathered in the corners of my eyes. I quietly relished this moment of being adorned and readied for the dance. Only an hour ago, they swept my hair into a French roll with tendrils dripping over my shoulder. I dabbed at my tears so the mascara would not run down my cheeks, marring the efforts of the women around me.

I wasn't preparing for a knight in shining armor or a prince charming. I had been asked to play the role of a heroine in a stage performance. My job was simple: allow other women to dress me, coif my hair, and apply my makeup. And then to waltz. I simply needed to match the strength of the hero with my poise as we danced on center stage.

The tears, held in check, were not from the stress. They were the effects of realizing that God had heard a secret dream of my heart.

A few months prior I was with friends, spouting off about life, and my secret slipped out.

"Just once, I wish I could go to a real ball and wear a real ball gown."

To me, the dream meant something far greater than dressing up. Rejection by an absent father created a dad-sized hole in my heart, and I longed to be a woman of whom dad would be proud. Like a little girl twirling in her princess dress whose awkward attempts catch the eye of her dad and put a twinkle in his eye, I too longed for the affirming look only a father can give.

At first I was a bit embarrassed; after all, the dream sounded juvenile for a young woman in her twenties. But regardless of what others thought, God listened and went to great lengths to make a tiny dream in my heart become a reality in my life.

Ball gowns and dances seemed so frivolous and shallow to me. But it seemed God saw them as a perfect opportunity to demonstrate his father-love. You see, I only asked for one occasion, but God gave me a five-night performance! For a short time each evening, I could fill up that dad-size emptiness and dance, knowing that my Heavenly Father watched with a twinkle in his eye, delighting in me.

What a lavish gift!

| Cheryl Meakins |

Take a Step

Take time today to do something that you delight in (sing in the shower, dance in the backyard) and reflect on the joy that Christ feels for you, his daughter.

Coffee Talk 13

Get together with one, two, or even more of your girlfriends, and celebrate your friendship. Here's stuff to do together.

★ Take time to share which of the devotions you read in the past few weeks was most meaningful to you, and why. It's OK if you all are at different places in the book—just share what God is putting on your heart.

★ Share an area of your life that you need your friends to be praying for you. And listen to the needs of your friends so you can pray for them. Remember to keep these confidential. Write each person's name and one word beside it to prompt you in prayer for her this week.

It's time to celebrate! You've made it through a year of devotions, a year of making time for God...and your girlfriends! Plan a special get-together at a local restaurant or coffee shop. Bring your books, and share your favorite devotions with one another. Celebrate how God (and your friends) have encouraged you through your times together.